THE BUDDHA'S TEACHINGS:

A GUIDE TO ATTAINING ENLIGHTENMENT

A LITERATURE REVIEW BASED ON SELECTED DISCOURSES FROM THE PALI CANON

BY

DR ARIYATHUSHEL ARAHANT

Chennai • Bangalore

CLEVER FOX PUBLISHING
Chennai, India

Published by CLEVER FOX PUBLISHING 2024
Copyright © Dr Ariyathushel Arahant 2024

All Rights Reserved.
ISBN: 978-93-56486-58-4

This book has been published with all reasonable efforts taken to make the material error-free after the consent of the author. No part of this book shall be used, reproduced in any manner whatsoever without written permission from the author, except in the case of brief quotations embodied in critical articles and reviews.

The Author of this book is solely responsible and liable for its content including but not limited to the views, representations, descriptions, statements, information, opinions and references ["Content"]. The Content of this book shall not constitute or be construed or deemed to reflect the opinion or expression of the Publisher or Editor. Neither the Publisher nor Editor endorse or approve the Content of this book or guarantee the reliability, accuracy or completeness of the Content published herein and do not make any representations or warranties of any kind, express or implied, including but not limited to the implied warranties of merchantability, fitness for a particular purpose. The Publisher and Editor shall not be liable whatsoever for any errors, omissions, whether such errors or omissions result from negligence, accident, or any other cause or claims for loss or damages of any kind, including without limitation, indirect or consequential loss or damage arising out of use, inability to use, or about the reliability, accuracy or sufficiency of the information contained in this book.

**Namo Tassa Bhagavato Arahato
Sammā Sambuddhassa!**

Homage to the Blessed One, the Worthy One,

the Supremely Enlightened One!

Preface

In presenting this work, I record my deepest sense of gratitude to all those who have contributed to preserve Buddha's teachings, including those who have contributed to sharing the teachings of Buddha by translating, editing and publishing the relevant materials related to Buddha's teachings in many ways.

Table of Contents

CHAPTER ONE: Introduction 7
CHAPTER TWO: Dhamma in Daily Life: Path towards Enlightenment 11
CHAPTER THREE: Stream Entry 15
CHAPTER FOUR: Ariya Sangha (Noble Sangha) 25
CHAPTER FIVE: Inner Qualities 32
CHAPTER SIX: Jhana Meditation Practice 39
CHAPTER SEVEN: Jhana Meditation Practice and Enlightenment (Nibbana) 45
CHAPTER EIGHT: Loving-Kindness Practice 48
CHAPTER NINE: Dhamma and Non-dhamma 52
CHAPTER TEN: Right View 55
CHAPTER ELEVEN: Supportive Factors for Enlightenment 59
CHAPTER TWELVE: Sensual Desires 62
CHAPTER THIRTEEN: The Four Noble Truths and Life Experiences 65
CHAPTER FOURTEEN: Everyday Life and Dhamma 68
CHAPTER FIFTEEN: Ten Fetters and Abandoning the Fetters 74
CHAPTER SIXTEEN: Right View and Good Dhamma 78
CHAPTER SEVENTEEN: Merits 81
CHAPTER EIGHTEEN: Life Goes in Cycles 85
CHAPTER NINETEEN: Dhamma Practice and Fruition 87
CHAPTER TWENTY: Stream Entry and Beyond 91
CHAPTER TWENTY-ONE: Arahathship 95
CHAPTER TWENTY-TWO: Further Thoughts 98
Sources 101

May all of the Noble wishes of those who read this book and practice Dhamma diligently be fulfilled, and may all beings be well and happy.

CHAPTER ONE:
Introduction

Buddha's teachings were founded and gifted to the world by Prince Siddhartha Gautama, known as "the Buddha", who lived more than 2,500 years ago in India. The word Buddha means "enlightened."

Prince Siddhartha, who was born a prince, decided to give up his lavish lifestyle, when, while in his twenties, he was moved by sufferings and began his search for enlightenment. After six years of searching, he attained enlightenment while meditating under a Bodhi tree. He spent the rest of his life teaching enlightenment. His teachings allowed several others to follow his path, to become his disciples and to attain enlightenment.

Enlightenment is a key aspect of Buddha's teachings and it is a peaceful mental state, which occurs due to the perfect understanding of the world as it really is. Such an understanding drives one to maintain wisdom combined with infinite compassion, joy and equanimity in all wakening states. In other words, by practicing Buddha's teachings to attain enlightenment, one becomes an independent, open-minded person who's kind, compassionate and joyful in all awakening states. Similarly, an enlightened person will gain a perfect unshakable balance of mind and will become a free person without attachments to worldly matters.

Buddha's teachings as a way of knowledge leads to liberation from suffering. Thus, the teachings of Buddha are extremely valuable because it eliminates sufferings. By attaining enlightenment or Nibbana, one can experience a blissful state in one's mind. The concepts of karma (the law of cause and effect) and samsara (cycle of death and rebirth) are common aspects taught by Buddha related to enlightenment. By attaining enlightenment, one can end all mental suffering and also the process of endless cycle of repeated birth and death.

Enlightenment was sought and attained by many people during Buddha's time, and those who practice Dhamma in line with Buddha's teachings can achieve enlightenment in present days. In general, all Buddhist practitioners strive to attain enlightenment and such an attainment is valuable because it eliminates sufferings. In essence, to attain enlightenment, one must gain an understanding of what Buddha has said and train one's mind in line with Buddha's teachings.

To gain theoretical understanding of what Buddha has said, it is beneficial to rely on the Pali Canon. Historical evidence suggests that the Pali Canon was preserved orally by the Sangha of Arahants during the first Buddhist council and continued through the second and third Buddhist councils in India. Although there were written texts available at the time of Buddha, an oral recounting was considered a more appropriate way of preserving the Buddha's original teachings. The first Buddhist council was held 30 years after the Parinibbana of the Buddha Gautama in India. The second Buddhist council occurred a century after the first, and the third Buddhist council was held during the reign of King Ashoka, India. During the fourth Buddhist council, which was held in Sri Lanka in the first century BCE, it was decided to write down the Pali Canon for the first time in history. These developments of the Pali Canon made it possible to preserve Buddha's teachings and to make them available for us to today.

The Pali Canon contains various Suttas taught by Buddha during his lifetime, and Buddha's original teachings can be located within the Pali Canon. Upon attaining enlightenment, one comes to realize that what is read in the Pali Canon or heard about Buddha's teachings based on the Pali Canon becomes one's personnel experience. Thus, the Pali Canon is the most reliable source available for practitioners to understand Buddha's teachings and to gain insight related to enlightenment, which is one of the key elements of Buddha's teachings.

The Sutta Pitaka of the Pali Canon is divided into five parts, called Nikayas. It contains more than 10,000 Sutta in the five Nikkayas or collections:

1. Digha Nikāya (the "long" discourses).
2. Majjhima Nikāya (the "middle-length" discourses).
3. Saṁyutta Nikāya (the "connected" discourses).
4. Anguttara Nikāya (the "numerical" discourses).
5. Khuddaka Nikāya (the "minor collection").

By recognizing the Pali Canon as the most important source available for understanding the authentic teachings of the Buddha, in this book, I attempt to provide an overview of Buddha's teachings related to the enlightenment based on selected discourses from the Sutta Pitaka of the Pali Canon. In this book, I have taken most of the Sutta quotes from the Anguttara Nikāya and the Khuddaka Nikāya. Some of the Sutta quotes are taken from the Majjhima Nikāya, Saṁyutta Nikāya, and the Digha Nikāya.

To gain a correct understanding of the path that leads to enlightenment and to understand how to practice Dharma in the correct way to attain enlightenment, understanding what Buddha actually taught is beneficial for practitioners. The aim of this book is to share the knowledge of Buddha's teachings with the reader. In doing so, this book seeks to explain the key themes related to enlightenment to the readers in a simple manner. In addition, I combine the theoretical knowledge from the Pali Canon with my penetrated knowledge of Dhamma to provide a guide to the reader about what enlightenment is and how to attain enlightenment in a simple manner.

The focus of this book is twofold. Firstly, it aims to provide an overview of what enlightenment is based on a literature review of the selected Suttas from the Pali Canon. Analysing some of the key themes emerging from the Sutta Pitaka of the Pali Canon can produce a summary of meaningful information emerging from the discourses of the Buddha. Secondly, this book aims to provide practical tips on how to attain enlightenment based on the insight knowledge that I gained during the process of my enlightenment experience. Overall, the book provides valuable information related to enlightenment based on Buddha's teachings. This book can help readers to understand the teachings of Buddha in a nutshell by filling the gap between the vast amount of Suttas and the relevant information scattered in the five Nikkayas of the Pali Canon on varied topics related to enlightenment, especially for readers who have some understanding of Buddha's teachings but who do not have the time, resources, and penetrated knowledge to fill that gap on their own. In this book, I have retained some of the Pali words (i.e Dhamma, sotapanna etc.) when it refers to the Buddha's teaching.

Buddha's teachings provide a uniform path to attain enlightenment, and all Arahants understand and teach the same Dhamma, which can be found in the Pali Canon. Since the content of the Sutta Pitaka becomes one's personal experience of enlightenment, I decided to quote Suttas from the Pali Canon to maintain Buddha's original teachings.

In essence, practitioners need the ability to understand the training methods that are described within the Pali Canon, and to do so, practitioners require expert Dhamma knowledge gained through penetrated knowledge to match the beginning and end of Dhamma phrases, understands its meaning well, and analyse the meaning to comprehend this Dhamma in the proper way. This may not be an easy task. This book serves to illustrate and produce training methods to attain enlightenment in simplified manner.

CHAPTER TWO:
DHAMMA IN DAILY LIFE: PATH TOWARDS ENLIGHTENMENT

Dhamma is to be practiced in daily life. By practicing Dhamma in daily life, one can gain success in all areas of life including worldly success and spiritual success.

Giving priority to Dhamma will indicate receiving success (and blessings) in all areas of life. See the following quotation, a passage of the Mahamangala Sutta as evidence of this matter:

"Ample learning, in crafts ability,
With a well-trained disciplining,
Well-spoken words, civility:
This, the Highest Blessing."

"Mother, father well supporting,
Wife and children duly cherishing,
Types of work unconflicting:
This, the Highest Blessing."

"Acts of giving, righteous living,
Relatives and kin supporting,
Actions blameless then pursuing:
This, the Highest Blessing."

"Avoiding evil and abstaining,
From besotting drinks refraining,

Diligence in Dhamma doing:
This, the Highest Blessing¹."

- Sn 2.4 (Mahamangala Sutta)

An enlightened person possesses a noble character and when a noble person is born, it is for benefit of all. A passage of the Sappurisa Sutta summarises as:

"Bhikkhus, when a good person is born in a family, it is for the good, welfare, and happiness of many people. It is for the good, welfare, and happiness of (1) his mother and father, (2) his wife and children, (3) his slaves, workers, and servants, (4) his friends and companions, and (5) ascetics and brahmins. Just as a great rain cloud, nurturing all the crops, appears for the good, welfare, and happiness of many people, so too, when a good person is born in a family."[2]

- AN 5.42 (Sappurisa Sutta)

A good person would care and look after everyone's wellbeing and becoming a good person will help one gets a step closer to attaining enlightenment. A passage of the Brahma Sutta summarises as:

"Mother and father are called 'Brahma,' and also 'first teachers.' They are worthy of gifts from their children, for they have compassion for their offspring. Therefore a wise person should revere them and treat them with honor. One should serve them with food and drink, with clothes and bedding, by massaging and bathing them, and by washing their feet. Because of that service to mother and father, the wise praise one in this world and after death one rejoices in heaven[3]."

- AN 4.63 (Brahma Sutta)

---

[1] Ref: "Maha-mangala Sutta: Protection" (Sn 2.4), translated from the Pali by Dr. R.L. Soni. *Access to Insight (BCBS Edition)*, 2013, Retrieved from: http://www.accesstoinsight.org/tipitaka/kn/snp/snp.2.04.soni.html
[2] Ref: Bhikkhu Bodhi (2012), AN 5.42(2) *The Good Person*, p.667.
[3] Ref: Bhikkhu Bodhi (2012), AN 4.63(3) *With Brahma*, p.454.

While engaging in normal daily activities, by practicing Dhamma diligently in line with Buddha's teachings, one can develop four factors of stream-entry, which are perfect confidence in Buddha, Dhamma, noble Sangha, and virtue that is agreeable to the noble ones.

Practicing in line with Buddha's teachings, one can attain enlightenment irrespective of lifestyles (monastic or lay) and other factors such as linage, gender, etc. See the following quotations as evident of this matter. The passages of the Dutiyajananakuhana Sutta and the Gihi Sutta record as:

"This holy life, as the path leading to ultimate freedom, was taught by the Blessed One only for the sake of realizing special knowledge, for attaining full understanding, and for avoiding dangers in this life and in future lives.

This noble path was always followed by the Great Sages. Those who follow this path exactly as taught by the Buddha, completely through the Buddha's message, will put an end to suffering".[4]

- Iti 36 (Dutiyajananakuhana Sutta)

"You should know, Sariputta, that any white-robed householder whose actions are restrained by five training rules and who gains at will, without trouble or difficulty, four pleasant visible dwellings that pertain to the higher mind, might, if he so wished, declare of himself: I am finished with hell, the animal realm, and the sphere of afflicted spirits; I am finished with the plane of misery, the bad destination, the lower world; I am a stream-enterer, no longer subject to [rebirth in] the lower world, fixed in destiny, heading for enlightenment!"[5]

- AN 5.179 (Gihi Sutta)

It has often been claimed that, to practice Dhamma in real life, one must give up worldly matters. However, giving up worldly matters

---

[4] Ref: "Dutiya Jananakuhana Sutta: Deceiving People 2", Iti 36, Itivuttaka, KN, Kiribathgoda Gananananda Thero, 2017, SuttaFriends.org, Retrieved from: https://suttafriends.org/sutta/itv36/
[5] Ref: Bhikkhu Bodhi (2012), AN 5.179 (9), *A Layman*, p.792.

indicates realizing that worldly matters are not permanent; they are subject to change and that worldly matters are non-self. By understanding the non-self-view, one will eliminate the stress experienced in daily life. Relieving stress will lead to getting more energy to perform daily activities with contentment, which will, in turn, result in gaining success in all areas of life.

Thus, giving up worldly matters to practice Dhamma does not indicate that one must give up worldly matters physically, because the physical world is created in the mind, and it is the giving up in the mind or non-attachment that is emphasized here. Therefore, a noble disciple is expected to grow in all areas of life, both materialistically and spiritually.

CHAPTER THREE:
STREAM ENTRY

Buddha's teachings are open to anyone regardless of whether one prefers to live in a house, a forest, or a monastery, and his teachings allow individuals to practice Dhamma based on their personal choices and lifestyles. By practicing Buddha's teachings, individuals can gain success in this life (both material and spiritual) and in the afterlife and also attain enlightenment if they wish. A passage of the story (Anandattherapanha Vatthu) related to the Dhammapada, Verses 54 and 55 record as:

"Ananda, supposing, there is one who takes refuge in the Three Gems (the Buddha, the Dhamma, the Samgha), who observes the five moral precepts, who is generous and not avaricious; such a man is truly virtuous and truly worthy of praise. The reputation of that virtuous one would spread far and wide, and bhikkhus, brahmins and laymen all alike would speak in praise of him, wherever he lives."[6]

It is possible to attain enlightenment by maintaining five precepts and developing daily life practices in line with Buddha's teachings while living a successful household life. By fulfilling duties and responsibilities towards others with kindness and compassion in daily life and practicing Dhamma diligently, one can experience peace. The path to enlightenment lies in one's ability to perform wholesome deeds. A passage of the Licchavi Kumāra Sutta summarises as:

"He always does his duty toward his parents; he promotes the welfare of his wife and children. He takes care of the people in his home and those who live in dependence on him.

---

[6] Ref: Daw Mya Tin, (1986), The Dhammapada: Verses and Stories.

The wise person, charitable and virtuous, acts for the good of both kinds of relatives, those who have passed away and those still living in this world.

[He benefits] ascetics and brahmins, and [also] the deities; he is one who gives rise to joy while living a righteous life at home.

Having done what is good, he is worthy of veneration and praise. They praise him here in this world and after death he rejoices in heaven[7]."

-AN 5.58 (Licchavi Kumāraka Sutta)

Typically, enlightenment is achieved and experienced through four progressive stages and these stages are:

1. Sotapanna (Stream-enterer)
2. Sakadagami (Once-returner)
3. Anagami (Non-returner)
4. Arahant

Each of these enlightenment stages is different as each stage eliminates different fetters. To learn about fetters, please see chapter fifteen of this book.

Ariya-puggala, (in Pali: "noble person") is a person who has attained one of the four levels of holiness. One becomes a Sotapanna, in the sense of being one who has irreversibly entered the "stream" that will ultimately lead him or her to full liberation by understanding what Buddha said. By realizing his teachings through direct knowledge, it is possible to proceed into the next stages of enlightenment.

Noble people are those individuals who have attained enlightenment irrespective of age, gender, dress, linage, dwelling, etc. A "change of lineage," occurs when an ordinary person becomes a noble person, and the noble linage is identified as the third in the Buddhist triad (Ariya-sangha) of Buddha. In other words, the Sangha of the Tathagata's disciples include the individuals who have attained enlightenment.

---

[7] Ref: Bhikkhu Bodhi (2012), AN 5.58(8), *Licchavi Youths*, p.692.

Buddha identified the noble linage as the best of the human clan because noble people uphold purified knowledge and pure moral conduct. They act for the welfare of others and are committed to being of service to all life. The voice of a noble person or listening to true Dhamma from a noble friend is a helpful factor to developing the right vision and to attaining enlightenment.

Stress is a common occurrence in life and stress can be caused by common life events which are difficult to avoid. When a person dissolves his or her inner tension through penetrated knowledge due to enlightenment, inner happiness and inner peace unfold on its own. By attaining enlightenment, one eliminates stress and the root cause of all stress, and mental sufferings. Thus, by eliminating stress and all mental sufferings, noble disciples of Buddha are expected to be energetic and grow or be successful in all areas of life. Please see the following quotation as evident of this matter, the Vaḍḍhi Sutta summarise as:

"Bhikkhus, growing in ten ways, a noble disciple grows by a noble growth, and he absorbs the essence and the best of this life. What ten? (1) He grows in fields and land; (2) in wealth and grain; (3) in wives and children; (4) in slaves, workers, and servants; (5) in livestock; (6) in faith; (7) virtuous behavior; (8) learning; (9) generosity, and (10) wisdom. Growing in these ten ways, a noble disciple grows by a noble growth, and he absorbs the essence and the best of this life."

"One who grows here in wealth and grain, in children, wives, and livestock, is wealthy and famous, honored by relatives and friends, and royalty."

"Such a discerning good man- who grows here in faith and virtous behaviour, in wisdom, generosity and learning—grows in both ways in this life."[8]

-AN 10.74 (Vaḍḍhi Sutta)

All people regardless of gender can attain the stages of enlightenment, for example, some of the relevant passages from the Paṭhamavaḍḍhi Sutta and Dutiyavaḍḍhi Sutta summarise as:

---

[8] Ref: Bhikkhu Bodhi (2012), AN 10.74. *Growth*, p.1430.

"Bhikkhus, growing in five ways, a male noble disciple grows by a noble growth, and he absorbs the essence and the best of this life. What five? He grows in faith, virtuous behavior, learning, generosity, and wisdom. Growing in these five ways, a male noble disciple grows by a noble growth, and he absorbs the essence and the best of this life."

"He who grows in faith and virtuous behavior, in wisdom, generosity, and learning—such a discerning superior man absorbs for himself the essence of this life."[9]

-AN 5.63 (Paṭhamavaḍḍhi Sutta)

"Bhikkhus, growing in five ways, a female noble disciple grows by a noble growth, and she absorbs the essence and the best of this life. What five? She grows in faith, virtuous behavior, learning, generosity, and wisdom. Growing in these five ways, a female noble disciple grows by a noble growth, and she absorbs the essence and the best of this life."

"She who grows in faith and virtuous behavior, in wisdom, generosity, and learning—such a virtuous female lay follower absorbs for herself the essence of this life."[10]

-AN 5.64 (Dutiyavaḍḍhi Sutta)

All people, regardless of their wealth, can attain the stages of enlightenment. See the following quotations as evident of this matter. The story associated with the Verses 50, Dhammapada (Paveyya ajivaka Vatthu) records as:

"A rich lady of Savatthi had adopted Paveyya, an ascetic, as a son and was looking after his needs. When she heard her neighbours talking in praise of the Buddha, she wished very much to invite him to her house to offer him alms-food. So, the Buddha was invited, and choice food was offered. As the Buddha was expressing appreciation

---
[9] Ref: Bhikkhu Bodhi (2012), AN 5.63 *Growth (1)*, p.693
[10] Ref: Bhikkhu Bodhi (2012), AN 5.64 *Growth (2)*, p.694

(*anumodana*), Paveyya, who was in the next room, fumed with rage. He blamed and cursed the lady for venerating the Buddha. The lady heard him cursing and shouting and felt so ashamed that she could not concentrate on what the Buddha was saying. The Buddha told her not to be concerned about those curses and threats, but to concentrate only on her own good and bad deeds.

Then the Buddha spoke in verse as follows:

Verse 50: One should not consider the faults of others, nor their doing or not doing good or bad deeds. One should consider only whether one has done or not done good or bad deeds.

At the end of the discourse the rich lady attained Sotapatti Fruition."[11]

- Dhammapada Verse 50

Dhammapada Verse 203 and Story (Eka Upasaka Vatthu) record as:

"One day, the Buddha saw in his vision that a poor man would attain Sotapatti Fruition at the village of Alavi. So he went to that village, which was thirty yojanas away from Savatthi. It so happened that on that very day the man lost his ox. So, he had to be looking for the ox. Meanwhile, alms-food was being offered to the Buddha and his disciples in a house in the village of Alavi. After the meal, people got ready to listen to the Buddha's discourse; but the Buddha waited for the young man. Finally, having found his ox, the man came running to the house where the Buddha was. The man was tired and hungry, so the Buddha directed the donors to offer food to him. Only when the man had been fed, the Buddha gave a discourse, expounding the Dhamma step by step and finally leading to the Four Noble Truths. The lay disciple attained Sotapatti Fruition at the end of the discourse.

---

[11]Ref: Daw Mya Tin, (1986), The Dhammapada: Verses and Stories.

Afterwards, the Buddha and his disciples returned to the Jetavana monastery. On the way, the bhikkhus remarked that it was so surprising that the Buddha should have directed those people to feed the young man before he gave the discourse. On hearing their remarks, the Buddha said, '*Bhikkhus! What you said is true, but you do not understand that I have come here, all this distance of thirty yojanas, because I knew that he was in a fitting condition to take in the Dhamma. If he were feeling very hungry, the pangs of hunger might have prevented him from taking in the Dhamma fully. That man had been out looking for his ox the whole morning and was very tired and also very hungry. Bhikkhus, after all, there is no ailment which is so difficult to bear as hunger.*'

Then the Buddha spoke in verse as follows:

Hunger is the greatest ailment, khandhas are the greatest ill. The wise, knowing them as they really are, realize Nibbana, the greatest bliss."[12]

-Dhammapada Verse 203

All people regardless of lifestyle (monastic or lay) can attain the stages of enlightenment. See the following quotations from the Dhammapada as evident of this matter.

The story associated with the Dhammapada, Verse 283 (Pancama-hallakabhikkhu Vatthu) *(and Verse 284)* record as:

"Once, in Savatthi, there were five friends who became bhikkhus only in their old age. These five bhikkhus were in the habit of going together to their old homes for alms-food. Of the former wives of those five, one lady in particular, by the name of Madhurapacika was a good cook and she looked after them very well. Thus, the five bhikkhus went mostly to her house. But one day, Madhurapacika fell ill and died suddenly. The old bhikkhus felt their loss very deeply and together they cried praising her virtues and lamenting their loss.

---

[12] Ref: Daw Mya Tin, (1986), The Dhammapada: Verses and Stories.

The Buddha called those bhikkhus to him and said, *'Bhikkhus! You all are feeling pain and sorrow because you are not free from greed, hatred, and ignorance (raga, dosa, moha), which are like a forest. Cut down this forest and you will be freed from greed, hatred and ignorance.'*

Then the Buddha spoke in verse as follows:

Verse 283: O bhikkhus, cut down the forest of craving, not the real tree; the forest of craving breeds danger (of rebirth). Cut down the forest of craving as well as its undergrowth and be free from craving.

At the end of the discourse the five old bhikkhus attained Sotapatti Fruition".[13]

-Dhammapada Verse 283

Dhammapada Verse 202 and Story (Annatarakuladarika Vatthu) record as:

"On the day a young woman was to be wedded to a young man, the parents of the bride invited the Buddha and eighty of his disciples for alms-food. Seeing the girl as she moved about the house, helping with the offering of alms-food, the bridegroom was very much excited, and he could hardly attend to the needs of the Buddha and the other bhikkhus. The Buddha knew exactly how the young bridegroom was feeling and also that time was ripe for both the bride and the bridegroom to attain Sotapatti Fruition.

By his supernormal power, the Buddha willed that the bride would not be visible to the bridegroom. When the young man could no longer see the young woman, he could pay full attention to the Buddha, and his love and respect for the Buddha grew stronger in him. Then the Buddha said to the young man, *'O young man, there is no fire like the fire of passion; there is no evil like anger and hatred; there is no ill like the burden of the five aggregates of existence (khandhas); there is no bliss like the Perfect Peace of Nibbana.'*

---

[13] Ref: Daw Mya Tin, (1986), The Dhammapada: Verses and Stories.

Then the Buddha spoke in verse as follows:

Verse 202: There is no fire like passion; there is no evil like hatred; there is no ill like (the burden of) khandhas; there is no bliss that surpasses the Perfect Peace (i.e., Nibbana).

At the end of the discourse both the bride and bridegroom attained Sotapatti Fruition[14]".

-Dhammapada Verse 202

Below is a quotation taken from the story associated with Dhammapada Verse 63 (Annatarakuladarika Vatthu) which records an incident related to two pick-pockets:

"On one occasion, two pick-pockets joined a group of lay-disciples going to the Jetavana monastery, where the Buddha was giving a discourse. One of them listened attentively to the discourse and soon attained Sotapatti Fruition. However, the second thief did not attend to the discourse as he was bent on stealing only; and he managed to snatch a small sum of money from one of the lay-disciples. After the discourse they went back and cooked their meal at the house of the second thief, the one who managed to get some money. The wife of the second thief taunted the first thief, 'You are so wise, you don't even have anything to cook at your house'. Hearing this remark, the first thief thought to himself, this one is so foolish that she thinks she is being very smart. Then, together with some relatives, he went to the Buddha and related the matter to him.

To the man, the Buddha spoke in verse as follows:

Verse 63: The fool who knows that he is a fool can, for that reason, be a wise man; but the fool who thinks that he is wise is, indeed, called a fool.

---

[14] Ref: Daw Mya Tin, (1986), The Dhammapada: Verses and Stories.

At the end of the discourse, all the relatives of the man attained Sotapatti Fruition."[15]

-Dhammapada Verse 63

It appears that some practitioners think it is the job of monks and nuns to practise and teach the Dharma and that it is the job of lay men and women to practise the Five Precepts and support the monks and nuns by providing them with their needs, this is an incorrect understanding. Buddha's intention was to develop a community of disciples, ordained and lay, men and women, who were well-educated in the Dhamma, who practised it fully to achieve enlightenment while supporting each other to both learn, develop and practice Dhamma irrespective of external factors such as dress code, lifestyle or lineage.

According to Buddha, the one who practices non-dhamma does not become monastic by merely living in a monastic setting. Similarly, one does not become a monastic by following a certain tradition, or by wearing a monastic dress, or by outside appearance, or by begging for food. One becomes monastic to the extent that one gains the true Dhamma knowledge through attaining enlightenment. See the following quotations as evidence of this matter, Dhammapada Verses 266 and 267 (Annatarabrahmana Vatthu) summarise as:

"Verse 266: He does not become a bhikkhu merely because he stands at the door for alms. He cannot become a bhikkhu because he acts according to a faith which is not in conformity with the Dhamma[16]."

"Verse 267: In this world, he who lays aside both good and evil, who leads the life of purity, and lives meditating on the khandha aggregates is indeed called a bhikkhu[17]."

-Dhammapada Verses 266 and 267

Noble linage exists out of mere rites and rituals. One who attains the stages of enlightenment will belong to the category of monastic or lay

---

[15] Ref: Daw Mya Tin, (1986), The Dhammapada: Verses and Stories.
[16] Ref: Daw Mya Tin, (1986), The Dhammapada: Verses and Stories.
[17] Ref: Daw Mya Tin, (1986), The Dhammapada: Verses and Stories.

based on their lifestyle not on mere rules and rituals or actual dwelling (monastery, house etc.). One who has achieved the higher stages of the enlightenment and lives the life of a monk (meaning maintaining celibacy) in a normal household will still be considered to be living the life of a monk who belongs to the noble community (Ariya Sangha) in line with Buddha's original teachings.

CHAPTER FOUR:
Ariya Sangha (Noble Sangha)

Buddha's noble disciples are those who have attained enlightenment at four stages (in Pali: Sotāpanna, Sakadāgāmi, Anāgāmi, and Arahant), please see the quote below as evidence to this matter:

"Bhikkhus, 'only here is there an ascetic, a second ascetic, a third ascetic, and a fourth ascetic [stream-winner, once returner, non-returner, or arahant]. The other sects are empty of ascetics.' It is in such a way that you should rightly roar your lion's roar."

- AN 4.241[18](Samaṇa Sutta)

Thus, the Buddha's true disciples included in the Triple Gem are those individuals who have experienced enlightenment at four stages (in Pali: Sotāpanna, Sakadāgāmi, Anāgāmi, and Arahant). In other words, this means the four types of noble disciples (or the eight types as individual types, including those who are on the path to enlightenment) are the Sangha included in the Triple gem.

The noble ones (Ariya Sangha) are good in their practice, upright in their practice, systematic in their practice and practicing Dhamma in the correct way. The noble ones having attained to right view will be free from self-view, doubts about Buddha, (and his teachings, Sangha), and attachment to rites and rituals. One who attains the first stage of enlightenment (Sotapanna) will be freed from the four planes of misery, and will no longer be born in the animal womb, or hell

---

[18] Ref: Bhikkhu Bodhi (2012), AN 4. 241(10), *Ascetics,* p.606.

realms or as a hungry ghost[19]. A quotation below from the Mahanama Sutta explaining the Sangha, a part of the Threefold Refuge records as:

"The Sahgha of the Blessed One's disciples is practicing the good, way, practicing the straight way, practicing the true way, practicing the proper way; that is, the four pairs of persons, the eight types of individuals— this Sangha of the Blessed One's disciples is worthy of gifts, worthy of hospitality, worthy of offerings, worthy of reverential salutation, the unsurpassed field of merit for the world."[20]

- AN 11.11 (Mahanama Sutta)

Numerous disciples of Buddha achieved enlightenment in the past and present days. There are three fetters that are fully eliminated by a Sotapanna and these three fetters are, non-self-view, doubts about Buddha, Dhamma and noble Sangha and attachment to rites and rituals. Below is a quotation taken from the Ratana Sutta as evident of this matter:

"As soon as one with insight is endowed, three things become discarded utterly: wrong view of a perduring self, and doubt, and clinging to vain rites and empty vows. Escaped that one from all four evil states, and of the six great sins incapable. Yea, in the Saṅgha is this glorious gem: By virtue of this truth, may blessing be![21]!"

- Snp 2.1 (The Threefold Gem)

The Buddha's goal was to have a community of disciples, who were well-educated in the Dharma from all kinds of communities, backgrounds and those who have chosen different lifestyles (monastic and lay). Noble Sangha or those who have attained enlightenment comes

---

[19] Beings take birth after birth in different planes of existence depending on their karma until they attain enlightenment. Noble disciples of Buddha are free of hell realms and other states of misery.
[20] Ref: Bhikkhu Bodhi (2012), AN 11.11(1) *Mahanama*, p.1566.
[21] Ref: Laurence Khantipalo Mills, (2015), *The Threefold Gem*, Sutta Nipāta, Published by SuttaCentral. p.78, Retrieved from: https://scdd.sfo2.cdn.digitaloceanspaces.com/uloads/orignal/2X/c/c289160d821380e41c5016120163a6c221a5b50e.pdf

from any setting (monastic or lay). One who has achieved the enlightenment (Arahathship) and free from moral defilements is called a "bhikkhu" an "arahant" irrespective of one's domicile.

Dhammapada Verse 142 summarises as:

"Though he is gaily decked, if he is calm, free from moral defilements, and has his senses controlled, if he is established in Magga Insight, if he is pure and has laid aside enmity (lit., weapons) towards all beings, he indeed is a brahmana, a samana, and a bhikkhu[22]."*

- Dhammapada Verse 142

Noble people choose their lifestyle based on their attainment of enlightenment and not merely based on rites and rituals. See for example, the quotation below taken from the Ghatikara Sutta which details about a noble Sangha member:

"The potter Ghatlkara has gone for refuge to the Buddha, the Dhamma, and the Sangha. He abstains from killing living beings, from taking what is not given, from misconduct in sensual pleasures, from false speech, and from wine, liquor, and intoxicants, which are the basis of negligence. He has perfect confidence in the Buddha, the Dhamma, and the Sangha, and he possesses the virtues loved by noble ones. He is free from doubt about suffering, about the origin of suffering, about the cessation of suffering, and about the way leading to the cessation of suffering. He eats only in one part of the day, he observes celibacy, he is virtuous, of good character. He has laid aside gems and gold, he has given up gold and silver. He does not dig the ground for clay using a pick with his own hand; what is left over from embankments or thrown up by rats, he brings home in a carrier; when he has made a pot he says: "Let anyone who likes set down some selected rice or selected beans or selected lentils, and let him take away whatever he likes. He supports his blind and aged Parents. Having de-

---

[22] Ref: Daw Mya Tin, (1986), The Dhammapada: Verses and Stories.
*The word brahmana meaning Arahant.

stroyed the five lower fetters, he is one who will reappear spontaneously (in the Pure Abodes) and there attain final Nibbana without ever returning from that world. [23]

-MN 81 (Ghatikara Sutta)

By entering the monastic order of a tradition, although one may commit to follow the Buddhist monastic way of life, that does not indicate that one automatically becomes enlightened to be included in the Buddha's' noble order. Evidence from the Pali Canon and other observations suggests that the noble order resides out of rites and rituals. It means that one can become a noble person by following a monastic lifestyle by choice in any setting (in a house, forest or monastery) but not necessarily entering a monastic order by following rites and rituals. Buddha's idea of a noble person means one who has purified inside and not the other factors. One becomes purified due to growth in wisdom and noble character that comes with enlightenment but not by following mere rites and rituals.

Similarly, Buddha rejects the idea of seniority in terms of years of Dhamma practice or memory of reciting, emphasizing instead the importance of realizing enlightenment, see for example, the quotations below from the Dhammapada Verse 19 and 20:

"Though he recites much the Sacred Texts (Tipitaka), but is negligent and does not practise according to the Dhamma, like a cowherd who counts the cattle of others, he has no share in the benefits of the life of a bhikkhu" [24]

(i.e., Magga-phala***)."

"Though he recites only a little of the Sacred Texts (Tipitaka), but practises according to the Dhamma, eradicating passion, ill will and ignorance, clearly comprehending the Dhamma, with his mind freed from moral defilements and no longer clinging to this world or to the

---

[23] Ref: Bhikkhu Bodhi (1995), "Ghatikara the Potter, Ghatikara Sutta, MN 81, p. 673-674.
[24] Ref: Daw Mya Tin, (1986), The Dhammapada: Verses and Stories.

next, he shares the benefits of the life of a bhikkhu[25] (i.e., Magga-phala)."

- Dhammapada Verses 19 and 20

Dhammapada Verses 262, 263 and Story (Sambahulabhikkhu Vatthu) about some Bhikkhus record as:

"At the monastery, young bhikkhus and samaneras were in the habit of attending on older bhikkhus who their teachers were. They washed and dyed the robes, or else performed other small services for their teachers. Some bhikkhus noticing these services envied those senior bhikkhus, and so they thought out a plan that would benefit them materially. Their plan was that they would suggest to the Buddha that young bhikkhus and samaneras should be required to come to them for further instruction and guidance even though they had been taught by their respective teachers. When they went to the Buddha with this proposal, the Buddha, knowing full well their motive, turned it down. To them the Buddha said, *'Bhikkhus I do not say that you are good-hearted just because you can talk eloquently. Only he who has got rid of covetousness and all that is evil by means of Arahatta Magga is to be called a good-hearted man.'*

Then the Buddha spoke in verse as follows:

Verse 262: Not by fine talk, nor by good looks could one be a good-hearted man, if he were envious, miserly and crafty.

Verse 263: A wise man who has cut off, uprooted and removed these and has rid himself of moral defilements is indeed called a good-hearted man."

- Dhammapada Verses 262 and 263[26]

Overall, Buddha's teaching is open to anyone from any background. See the following quotations from the Dhammapada as evident of this matter.

---

[25] Ref: Daw Mya Tin, (1986), The Dhammapada: Verses and Stories.
[26] Ref: Daw Mya Tin, (1986), The Dhammapada: Verses and Stories.

Dhammapada Verse 283 and Story (Pancamahallakabhikkhu Vatthu) records as:

"Once, in Savatthi, there were five friends who became bhikkhus only in their old age. These five bhikkhus were in the habit of going together to their old homes for alms-food. Of the former wives of those five, one lady in particular, by the name of Madhurapacika was a good cook and she looked after them very well. Thus, the five bhikkhus went mostly to her house. But one day, Madhurapacika fell ill and died suddenly. The old bhikkhus felt their loss very deeply and together they cried praising her virtues and lamenting their loss.

The Buddha called those bhikkhus to him and said, *'Bhikkhus! You all are feeling pain and sorrow because you are not free from greed, hatred, and ignorance (raga, dosa, moha), which are like a forest. Cut down this forest and you will be freed from greed, hatred and ignorance.'*

Then the Buddha spoke in verse as follows:

Verse 283: O bhikkhus, cut down the forest of craving, not the real tree; the forest of craving breeds danger (of rebirth). Cut down the forest of craving as well as its undergrowth and be free from craving. At the end of the discourse the five old bhikkhus attained Sotapatti Fruition[27]".

- Dhammapada Verses 283

Dhammapada Verse 202 and Story (Annatarakuladarika Vatthu) record as:

"On the day a young woman was to be wedded to a young man, the parents of the bride invited the Buddha and eighty of his disciples for alms-food. Seeing the girl as she moved about the house, helping with the offering of alms-food, the bridegroom was very much excited, and he could hardly attend to the needs of the Buddha and the other bhikkhus. The Buddha knew exactly how the young bridegroom was feeling and also that time was ripe for both the bride and the bridegroom

---

[27] Ref: Daw Mya Tin, (1986), The Dhammapada: Verses and Stories.

to attain Sotapatti Fruition. By his supernormal power, the Buddha willed that the bride would not be visible to the bridegroom. When the young man could no longer see the young woman, he could pay full attention to the Buddha, and his love and respect for the Buddha grew stronger in him.

Then the Buddha said to the young man, '*O young man, there is no fire like the fire of passion; there is no evil like anger and hatred; there is no ill like the burden of the five aggregates of existence (khandhas); there is no bliss like the Perfect Peace of Nibbana.*'

Then the Buddha spoke in verse as follows:

Verse 202: There is no fire like passion; there is no evil like hatred; there is no ill like (the burden of) khandhas; there is no bliss that surpasses the Perfect Peace (i.e., Nibbana).

At the end of the discourse both the bride and bridegroom attained Sotapatti Fruition[28]".

- Dhammapada Verse 202

Upon attaining enlightenment, irrespective of whether one leaves the physical home to live in a monastery or not, one becomes a noble person because enlightenment happens in a mental level. Irrespective of where one resides, whether in a monastic setting, a forest or a house, by practicing Dhamma in the correct way as proclaimed by Buddha, one can become enlightened. The enlightened people are the true disciples of Buddha who are practicing Dhamma in the correct way and they are the third of the three Gems.

---

[28] Ref: Daw Mya Tin, (1986), The Dhammapada: Verses and Stories.

CHAPTER FIVE:
INNER QUALITIES

In his Disciples' teachings, Buddha has appreciated the wise realization of Dhamma and the inner qualities of a person that makes one a noble character. The word "Bhikku" in Pali would indicate someone who begs. As described by certain Suttas, a "Bhikku" can practice Dhamma rightly or wrongly. The "Bhikku" who practice Dhamma in the correct way may become an "Ariya-puggala" or a nobel person to be included in the Sangha of Triple Gem. See the following quotation from the Yathābhata sutta as evidence of this matter.

"Bhikkhus, possessing five qualities, a bhikkhu is deposited in hell as if brought there. What five? Here, a bhikkhu is devoid of faith, morally shameless, morally reckless, lazy; and unwise. Possessing these five qualities, a bhikkhu is deposited in hell as if brought there."

"Bhikkhus, possessing five [other] qualities, a bhikkhu is deposited in heaven as if brought there. What five? Here, a bhikkhu is endowed with faith, has a sense of moral shame, has moral dread, and is energetic and wise. Possessing these five qualities, a bhikkhu is deposited in heaven as if brought there[29]."

-AN 5.4 (Yathābhata Sutta)

Upon attaining the first stage of enlightenment, one will eliminate three fetters, including non-self-view.

---

[29] Ref: Bhikkhu Bodhi (2012), AN 5.4(4) *As If Brought There*, p.631.

A relevant passage of the Sabhiya Sutta summarise as:

"Sabhiya:

Attaining what is one called a bhikkhu?
How is one gentle? And how tamed?
Why is one called awakened?
Please answer me this question, Lord.

Buddha:

By the path they walked themselves,
Nirvāṇa is realized and doubt is left behind;
Existence and non-existence have been abandoned,
Complete, having ended rebirth: they are a bhikkhu.

Mindful and equanimous everywhere,
They do not harm anyone in the world;
An ascetic crossed over, without distress,
And with no vanity: they are gentle.

With faculties developed
For the whole world, inside and out;
They have understood this world and the next,
And complete their time fulfilled: they are tamed.

Having thoroughly investigated the ages
Of transmigration through both deaths and births,
Free of passion and defilements, pure,
Arrived at the end of rebirth:
Such is called awakened.[30]"

-Snp 3.6 (Sabhiya Sutta)

---

[30] Ref: "Sabhiya Sutta: Sabhiya's Questions", Snp 3.6, Sutta Nipāta, translated by Pali from Bhikku Sujato (2021), SuttaCentral. Retrieved from: https://suttacentral.net/snp3.6/en/sujato

Dhammapada Verses 262 and 263 record as:

"Verse 262: Not by fine talk, nor by good looks could one be a good-hearted man, if he were envious, miserly and crafty[31]."

"Verse 263: A wise man who has cut off, uprooted and removed these and has rid himself of moral defilements is indeed called a good-hearted man[32]."

-Dhammapada Verses 262 and 263

A passage of the Huhuṅka Sutta summarises as:

"Any brahman who has banished evil qualities, –not overbearing, not stained, his mind controlled–gone to the end of wisdom, the holy life completed: Rightly would that brahman speak the holy teaching. He has no swelling of pride anywhere in the world[33]".

-Ud 1.4 (Huhuṅka Sutta)

An individual who attains the first stage of enlightenment (Sotapanna) possesses confidence (gained through insight) in Buddha, Dhamma, and noble Sangha (at the same time, three fetters are removed at once, i.e., non-self-view, doubts, attachment to rites, and rituals).

The enlightened person has a deep reverence for all living beings. Moreover, the enlightened person is joyful, kind and is willing to share that joy and kindness with others. The realization of four noble truths through direct knowledge will transform an individual to have good attitudes that he or she will abstain from unwholesome conduct but perform wholesome conduct while fulfilling responsibilities in all areas of life, with generosity, loving-kindness, and compassion towards everyone. When performing daily activities in a rigorous man-

---

[31] Ref: Daw Mya Tin, (1986), The Dhammapada: Verses and Stories.
[32] Ref: Daw Mya Tin, (1986), The Dhammapada: Verses and Stories.
[33] Ref: "Overbearing: Huhuṅka Sutta", Ud 1:4, KN, Translated from Pali by Thanissaro Bhikkhu (2012), dhammatalks.org. Retrieved from: https://www.dhammatalks.org/suttas/KN/Ud/ud1_4.html

ner, happiness will flow into one's mind and will lead to joy and concentration, which in turn will help one to develop further in the path leading to Arahanthship.

Upon attaining Anagami state and thereby abandoning sensual desires (and ill will), typically, one would abandon household life into homelessness (mentally), however, this may not be possible (physically) for everyone due to circumstances like the poter Ghatlkara (and the context). In such cases, noble persons will continue to live a life like a monk with restrained sense-faculties due to the removal of fetters irrespective of where they live (in a house, monastery, or forest). This transformation happens not because one following rules but because one has eliminated the desire for sensual desires due to understanding non-self-view.

About context, going from home to homelessness during Buddha's time would have indicated meeting Buddha and joining the Sangha of monks who mainly belonging to the noble order. The context has changed over time.

By understanding what the Buddha has actually said, one will be able to make progress in the path of enlightenment and to experience peace within or Nibbana. In other words, a noble person becomes a monk by conduct due to gaining insight knowledge. Essentially that means one maintains the noble qualities of a person in all wakening states. Therefore, from an enlightenment perspective, those who want to attain enlightenment will benefit by reflecting the qualities in Buddha, Dhamma, and noble Sangha while cultivating wholesome conducts in daily life to become a person of noble character. The Thera Sutta describes the qualities that make one an Arahant:

"This is as I heard from the Blessed One. At one time the Blessed One was staying in the province of Sāvatthī, at Jeta's garden, in Anāthapiṇḍika's monastery. That day, Arahant Sāriputta, Arahant Mahā Moggallāna, Arahant Mahā Kassapa, Arahant Mahā Kaccāyana, Arahant Mahā Koṭṭhata, Arahant Mahā Kappina, Arahant Mahā Cunda, Arahant Anuruddha, Arahant Revata and Arahant Nanda were approaching the Blessed One. Seeing those liberated monks coming in the distance the Blessed One told the monks who were with him, "Oh monks, there comes Brāhmins, oh monks, there comes Brāhmins."

At that time, a certain monk who was from the Brāhmin clan asked the Blessed One, 'Oh Blessed One, how does one become a Brāhmin? What are the qualities that make one a Brāhmin? '

Then, the Blessed One who realised the true nature as it really is spoke the following inspired verse,

Those who have discarded all evil, live always with clear mindfulness, have destroyed the bonds of rebirths, and have realised the four noble truths are truly Brāhmins in the world."[34]*

-Ud 1.5 T (Thera Sutta)

Dhammapada Verse 393 summarises as:

"Not by wearing matted hair, nor by lineage, nor by caste, does one become a brahmana; only he who realizes the Truth and the Dhamma is pure; he is a brahmana[35].".

- Dhammapada Verse 393

The story associated with the Dhammapada Verse 394 (Kuhakabrahmana Vatthu) records as:

"Once, a deceitful brahmin climbed up a tree near the city-gate of Vesali and kept himself hanging upside down like a bat from one of the branches of the tree. From this very awkward position, he kept on muttering, "O people! Bring me a hundred heads of cattle, many pieces of silver and a number of slaves. If you do not bring these to me, and if I were to fall down from this tree and die, this city of yours will surely come to ruin." The people of the town, fearing that their city night be destroyed if the brahmin were to fall down and die,

---

[34] *The word Brahmins means Arahants.
Ref: "Thera Sutta: The Liberated Ones", Ud 1.5, Udāna, Kiribathgoda Gananada Thero, 2017, SuttaFriends.org. Retrieved from: https://suttafriends.org/sutta/ud1-5/
[35] Ref: Daw Mya Tin, (1986), The Dhammapada: Verses and Stories.

brought all the things he demanded and pleaded with him to come down.

The bhikkhus hearing about this incident reported to the Buddha and the Buddha replied that the deceitful one could only cheat the ignorant people but not the wise ones."

Then the Buddha spoke in verse as follows:

Verse 394: O foolish one! What is the use of wearing matted hair? What is the use of your wearing a garment made of antelope skin? In you, there is a forest (of moral defilements); you clean yourself only externally[36]".

-Dhammapada Verse 394

The noble eightfold path consists of eight practices and include: right view, right resolve, right speech, right conduct, right livelihood, right effort, right mindfulness, and right samadhi (meditative absorption or concentration). By practicing the noble eightfold path, one can attain enlightenment. To practice the noble eightfold path in the correct way, one must gain the right understanding of what Buddha taught by attaining at least the first stage of enlightenment that is Sotapanna. One who gains the right view at the first stage of enlightenment is capable in practicing the noble eightfold path in the correct way. Thus, one who attains the first stage of enlightenment is guaranteed to become an Arahant. For those who wish to attain enlightenment, it will be beneficial to put extra efforts in attaining the first stage of enlightenment. A passage of the Mahā Parinibbāna Sutta summarises as:

"In any doctrine & discipline where the noble eightfold path is not ascertained, no contemplative of the first... second... third... fourth order [stream-winner, once-returner, non-returner, or arahant] is ascertained. But in any doctrine & discipline where the noble eightfold path is ascertained, contemplatives of the first... second... third... fourth order are ascertained.

---

[36] Ref: Daw Mya Tin, (1986), The Dhammapada: Verses and Stories.

The noble eightfold path is ascertained in this doctrine & discipline, and right here there are contemplatives of the first… second… third… fourth order. Other teachings are empty of knowledgeable contemplatives. And if the monks dwell rightly, this world will not be empty of arahants.[37]

-DN16 (Mahā Parinibbāna Sutta)

In summary, enlightenment is accessible to those who follow the Buddha's teachings. Given that enlightenment is happening at the mental level, the outside appearance is not a contributory factor.

Buddha's teaching provides a uniform path leading to enlightenment and all Arahants understand and show the same path. The first stage of enlightenment is usually achieved by listening to true Dhamma from noble persons. For those who are interested, it is now possible to hear Dhamma from noble people.

---

[37] Ref: "Mahā Parinibbāna Sutta: The Great Total Unbinding Discourse", DN 16, Translated from Pali by Thanissaro Bhikkhu (2017), dhammatalks.org. Retrieved from: https://www.dhammatalks.org/suttas/DN/DN16.html

CHAPTER SIX:
Jhana Meditation Practice

There are four stages of enlightenment and these four stages are:
1. Sotapanna (Stream-enterer)
2. Sakadagami (Once-returner)
3. Anagami (Non-returner)
4. Arahant

At each stage of the enlightenment, one eliminated the relevant fetters. Typically, the path has a gradual development.

The Sotapanna or the stream-enterer stage meaning 'one who enters the stream', with the 'stream' being the noble eightfold path. The stream-enterer has the perfect understanding of the Buddha, and his teachings. Thus, at Sotapanna stage, one eliminates three mental fetters which are self-view, doubt of Buddha, Dhamma and noble Sangha, and attachments to rites and rituals including wrong practices. At Anagami level, one eliminates sensual desire and ill will.

Jhanas play a role in enlightenment. Jhana refers to unified concentration on a meditative object. Jhana practice is needed to achieve the higher stages of enlightenment but in reality, jhanas come to establish naturally in the mind of a practitioner due to insight of non-self-view gained at the Sotapanna level.

Jhana include rūpa jhānas and arūpa-jhānas.

Rūpa jhānas are of four kinds:

1. First jhāna: A medicant experiences rapture (pīti) and pleasure (non-sensual sukha) as the result of seclusion and right effort, discursive thought (vitarka-vicara) continues.

2. Second jhāna: A medicant experiences rapture (pīti) and pleasure (non-sensual sukha) as the result of the result of concentration (samadhi-ji, "born of samadhi"); unification of awareness (ekaggata) free from discursive thought (vitarka-vicara); inner tranquility (sampasadana).
3. Third jhāna: A medicant experiences equanimous (upekkhā), mindful, and alert, and senses pleasure with the body.
4. Fourth jhāna: A medicant experiences purity of equanimity and mindfulness (upekkhāsatipārisuddhi), neither-pleasure-nor-pain.

The four arūpa-jhānas are:

1. Fifth jhāna: Infinite space
2. Sixth jhāna: Infinite consciousness
3. Seventh jhāna: Infinite nothingness
4. Eighth jhāna: Neither perception nor non-perception

Initially, by practicing precepts or rules and by temporarily abandoning the five hindrances (sense desire, ill-will etc.), one could develop jhana or deep concentration. However, to attain enlightenment, one must eliminate the root cause of sensual desire through gaining the insight of non-self-view.

Typically, jhanas are experienced at the third stage of enlightenment (i.e Anagami) and that is after eliminating the first three fetters (self-view, doubts about Buddha, his teachings, and noble Sangha, attachment to rites and rituals).

Right view is gained at the first stage of enlightenment, and three fetters are at once abandoned, because removing the doubts about Buddha and his teachings (thereby not mixing outsiders' teaching into Buddha's teaching) along with non-self-view are essential for the attainment of enlightenment. Jhana or the concentrative state should be developed alongside the right view to attain the enlightenment.

Jhana or the concentrative state would come under the right concentration, which is the eighth factor in the Noble Eightfold Path, should accompany by the right view (first factor in the Noble Eightfold Path) to attain enlightenment.

Therefore, to attain enlightenment or, in other words, to become an Arahant, the correct practice requires that one gain the right view through insight knowledge, the first factor of the Noble Eightfold Path to complete experience with Jhana to attain the final stage of enlightenment.

The teachings that can be found in Suttas become the personal experiences of all Arahants, as they all understand the same thing. Right practice leads to blissful Nibbana and knowing what is the right practice can be beneficial for those who are seeking it.

Please see the quotation below from the Paṭhama-taj-jhāna Sutta which describes that one needs to eliminate six things to experience the first jhana:

"Bhikkhus, without having abandoned six things, one is incapable of entering and dwelling in the first jhana. What six?

Sensual desire, ill will, dullness and drowsiness, restlessness and remorse, doubt; and one has not clearly seen with correct wisdom, as it really is, the danger in sensual pleasures. Without having abandoned these six things, one is incapable of entering and dwelling in the first jhana.

Bhikkhus, having abandoned six things, one is capable of entering and dwelling in the first jhana. What six?

Sensual desire, ill will, dullness and drowsiness, restlessness and remorse, doubt; and one has clearly seen with correct wisdom, as it really is, the danger in sensual pleasures. Having abandoned these six things, one is capable of entering and dwelling in the first jhana[38]."

-AN 6.73 (Paṭhama-taj-jhāna)

---

[38] Ref: Bhikkhu Bodhi (2012), AN 6.73 (9), *First Jhana (1)*, p.972.

At the preliminary stage in the path to Sotapanna or the first stage of enlightenment, it is beneficial to lay a foundation of moral disciplines as the moral discipline will lead to concentration which will allow one to investigate true Dhamma (and to develop wisdom). Upon attaining the first stage of enlightenment, one will naturally behave with morals due to insight without needing to observe precepts as rules. Furthermore, for those who aspire to attain enlightenment, as a form of training, it will be beneficial to combine the practice of reflect on non-self-view in daily life and the qualities of Buddha, Dhamma, and noble Sangha to eliminate the first three fetters and to gain the non-self-view. At the third stage of enlightenment, one will eliminate the lower fetters including sensual desires and ill will.

Although meditative concentration (jhanas) can be developed in the minds of practitioners due to intense meditation without gaining the right view and thereby without having eliminated the first three fetters (self-view, doubts about Buddha, Dhamma and noble Sangha, rites, and rituals) and the subsequent two fetters (ill will and sensual pleasures) rightly, such practice will not lead to enlightenment because it is not possible to become an Arahant without having the right view and understanding what the Buddha has said through insight knowledge.

Please see below a quotation taken from the Vihāra Sutta:

"Bhikkhus, there are these nine progressive dwellings. What nine? (1) Here, secluded from sensual pleasures, secluded from unwholesome states, a bhikkhu enters and dwells in the first jhana, which consists of rapture and pleasure born of seclusion, accompanied by thought and examination. (2) With the subsiding of thought and examination, he enters and dwells in the second jhana, which has internal placidity and unification of mind and consists of rapture and pleasure born of concentration, without thought and examination. (3) With the fading away as well of rapture, he dwells equanimous and, mindful and clearly comprehending, he experiences pleasure with the body; he enters and dwells in the third jhana of which the noble ones declare: He is equanimous, mindful, one who dwells happily. (4) With the abandoning of pleasure and pain, and with the previous passing away of joy and dejection, he enters and dwells in the fourth jhana, neither painful nor pleasant, which has purification of mindfulness by equanimity. (5) With the complete surmounting of perceptions of forms, with the passing away of perceptions of sensory impingement, with non-attention to perceptions of diversity, [perceiving] space is infinite/ a bhikkhu enters and dwells in the base of the infinity of space. (6) By completely surmounting the base of the infinity of space, [perceiving] consciousness is infinite/ he enters and dwells in the base of the infinity of consciousness. (7) By completely surmounting the base of the infinity of consciousness, [perceiving] there is nothing/ he enters and dwells in the base of nothingness. (8) By completely surmounting the base of nothingness, he enters and dwells in the base of neither- perception-nor-non-perception. (9) By completely surmounting the base of neither-perception-nor-non-perception, he enters and dwells in the cessation of perception and feeling. These, bhikkhus, are the nine progressive dwellings[39]."

- AN 9.32 (Vihāra Sutta)

By attaining enlightenment, one can eliminate all stress and sufferings, and it brings relief to those who need it. A passage of the Ajāta Sutta summarises as:

"The escape from the five groups of clinging is absolutely peaceful, beyond reasoning, permanent, unborn, unproduced, sorrowless, and stainless. Nibbāna, the ultimate freedom, is the cessation of all suffering. There, the stilling of all conditioned things is extremely blissful[40]."

-Itv 43 (Ajāta Sutta)

Thus, those who aspire to attain enlightenment will benefit from reflecting the qualities of Buddha to eliminate the first three fetters and to proceed to higher stages of enlightenment. Wise people will understand the teachings of Buddha and will end their sufferings by eliminating self-view. A passage of the Vipallāsa Sutta summarises as:

---

[39] Ref: Bhikkhu Bodhi (2012), AN 9.32(1), *Dwellings (1)*, p.1287-1288.

[40] Ref: "Ajāta Sutta: The Unborn", Itv 43, Itivuttaka, Kiribathgoda Ganananda Thero (2017), Suttafriends.org. Retrieved from: https://suttafriends.org/sutta/itv43/

"But when the Buddhas arise in the world, sending forth a brilliant light, they reveal this Dhamma that leads to the stilling of suffering.

Having heard it, wise people have regained their sanity. They have seen the impermanent as impermanent and what is suffering as suffering.

They have seen what is non-self as non-self and the unattractive as unattractive. By the acquisition of right view, they have overcome all suffering[41]".

-AN 4.49 (Vipallāsa Sutta)

---

[41] Ref: Bhikkhu Bodhi (2012), AN 4.49 (9), *Inversions*, p.438.

CHAPTER SEVEN:
Jhana Meditation Practice and Enlightenment (Nibbana)

Jhanas are temporary meditative states in the mind, but the effect of Nibbana indicates the complete cessation of cravings and freedom from stress experienced during all waking states.

Formless Jhanas (meditative concentrations) in isolation can be achieved by the practitioners through intense meditation practice. Such attainments of Jhanas in isolation will not lead to Nibbana.

When an individual practice in line with Buddha's teaching, typically, one will experience jhanas after attaining the Anagami stage (with removal of two fetters: sensual desires and ill will) and essentially after removing the three fetters at the Sotapanna stage (i.e self-view, doubts about Buddha, Dhamma and Sangha, attachment for rites, and rituals).

A passage of the Yodhajiva Sutta summarises as:

"Having abandoned these five hindrances, defilements' of the mind that weaken wisdom, secluded from sensual pleasures, secluded from unwholesome states, he enters and dwells in the first jhana ... the fourth jhana, neither painful nor pleasant, which has purification of mindfulness by equanimity."

"When his mind is thus concentrated, purified, cleansed, unblemished, rid of defilement, malleable, wieldy, steady, and attained to imperturbability, he directs it to the knowledge of the destruction of the taints. He understands as it really is: 'This is suffering'. He understands as it really is: 'This is the origin of suffering'. He understands as it really is: 'This is the cessation of suffering'. He understands as it really is: 'This is the way leading to the cessation of suffering'. He understands as it really is: These are the taints. He understands as it really is: 'This is the origin of the taints'. He understands as it really is: 'This is the cessation of the taints'. He understands as it really is: 'This is the way leading to the cessation of the taints'. When he knows and sees thus, his mind is liberated from the taint of sensual desire, from the taint of existence, and from the taint of ignorance. When it is liberated, there comes the knowledge: '[It's] liberated'. He understands: 'Destroyed is birth, the spiritual life has been lived, what had to be done has been done, there is no more coming back to any state of being'.[42]"

- AN 5.75 (Yodhajiva Sutta)

A passage of the Santatara Sutta summarises as:

"Monks, the formless jhana is more peaceful than the form jhana and Nibbāna is still more peaceful than the formless jhana.

This is the meaning of what the Blessed One said. So, with regard to this, it was said:

Some are born in the form realm and others are born in the formless realm. They have not attained Nibbāna and so they return to renewed existence.

Those who fully understand the form realm and those who free their minds from the formless realm are released based on Nibbāna. The liberated one defeats the army of Mara, the evil one.

The fully enlightened Buddha has touched Nibbāna with his body and is free from defilements.

Having abandoned all taints, the Buddha teaches the sorrowless, stainless state, Nibbāna[43]."

-Itv 73 (Santatara Sutta)

---

[42] Ref: Ref: Bhikkhu Bodhi (2012), AN 5.75 (5) *Warriors,* p.703-704.
[43] Ref: "Santatara Sutta: More Peaceful", Itv 73, Itivuttaka, Kiribathgoda Gananande Thero (2017), Suttafriends.org. Retrieved from: https://suttafriends.org/sutta/itv73/

Typically, Arahants can enter into states of absorption (jhanas) at any time they wish and also experience "Nirodha Samapatti" (attainment of extinction), a state of temporary suspension of all mental activity. Nibbana is a blissful state than achieving the jhanas. Nibbana is experienced at four stages (Sotapanna, Sakadagami, Anagami and Arahant).

An individual who attains the stage of Sotapanna will certainly achieve Arahatship at some point, although time may vary between individuals (it can happen within the very next moment to next day or next year to a maximum of 7 births). Thus, for those who are interested in achieving enlightenment, it will be beneficial to put extra effort to achieve the stage of Sotapanna.

To attain enlightenment, one must abandon ten fetters. The first three fetters are the identity view, doubts about Buddha, his teachings and his noble disciples, and attachment for rites and rituals. These three fetters are abandoned at the first stage of enlightenment. Those who have doubts about Buddha or his teachings will not be able to abandon the first three fetters to attain enlightenment. Therefore, in essence, one who wants to attain enlightenment will benefit from practicing Dhamma as proclaimed by Buddha. Listening to true Dhamma from noble people and practicing in line with Dhamma as proclaimed by Buddha will bring great benefits to those who want to achieve the first stage of enlightenment or Sotapanna.

CHAPTER EIGHT:
LOVING-KINDNESS PRACTICE

Metta Sutta (Discourse on loving-kindness) is one of the popular Suttas and it guides what one should do if wanting to achieve peace (or Nibbana). It explains that one must try and maintain certain practices (be able, upright, straight and not proud, easy to speak to, mild and well content, easily satisfied, not caught up in too much busy life, etc.) to find peace within or experience Nibbana.

By cultivating and practicing good qualities as mentioned in Metta Sutta, one can become a good person, to begin with, and, essentially, the path to Nibbana requires that one become a good person while living a day-to-day life to become a noble person towards the end of the path as it is a progressive path.

Similarly, loving-kindness meditation is one of the popular meditation practices. Although beginners may continue to practice loving-kindness as a form of meditation limiting the practice to a comfortable time (may it be 15 minutes, 30 minutes per day or hours based on personal preference), to advance into the path of Nibbana, one must maintain loving-kindness in all waking states in day-to-day life, as this is the mental state of an Arahant.

Along with the right view gained (the right view is gained by attaining the first stage of enlightenment at the Sotapanna stage), if one continues to maintain loving-kindness in daily life and throughout waking hours, this practice will help one eliminate ill will along with sensual desires at the Anagami state and to become an Arahant. In practice, by combining the right view to loving-kindness practice in daily life, one will be able to progress in the path of enlightenment.

For those who wish to attain Nibbana, it will be useful to develop and practice loving-kindness through all wakening states in their daily lives and to gain the right view by listening to true Dhamma from noble people or in other words, from people who have attained enlightenment.

A passage of the Karaniya Metta Sutta summarises as:

"Let none deceive another,
    Or despise any being in any state.
Let none through anger or ill-will
    Wish harm upon another.
Even as a mother protects with her life
    Her child, her only child,
So with a boundless heart
    Should one cherish all living beings;
Radiating kindness over the entire world:
    Spreading upwards to the skies,
And downwards to the depths;
    Outwards and unbounded,
Freed from hatred and ill-will.
    Whether standing or walking, seated or lying down
Free from drowsiness,
    One should sustain this recollection.
This is said to be the sublime abiding.
    By not holding to fixed views,
The pure-hearted one, having clarity of vision,
    Being freed from all sense desires,
Is not born again into this world...[44]"

-Sn 1.8 (Karaniya Metta Sutta)

The path to enlightenment lies in one's ability to performing wholesome deeds. By fulfilling duties and responsibilities towards others with kindness and compassion, one can experience peace. Most of these qualities can be found in the famous Karaṇīya Mettā-Sutta that

---

[44] Ref: "Karaniya Metta Sutta: The Buddha's Words on Loving-Kindness" (Sn 1.8), translated by the Amaravati Sangha, Accesstoinsight.Org. Retrieved from: www.accesstoinsight.org/tipitaka/kn/snp/snp.1.08.amar.html

provides a guideline on how one can practice attaining Nibbana or peace within and similar guidelines can be found in several other Suttas including Mangala Sutta.

Mettānisamsa Sutta detail the benefits of practicing loving-kindness, see the quotation below:

"Bhikkhus, when the liberation of the mind by loving-kindness has been pursued, developed, and cultivated, made a vehicle and basis, carried out, consolidated, and properly undertaken, eleven benefits are to be expected. What eleven? (1) One sleeps well; (2) one awakens happily; (3) one does not have bad dreams; (4) one is pleasing to human beings; (5) one is pleasing to spirits; (6) deities protect one; (7) fire, poison, and weapons do not injure one; (8) one's mind quickly becomes concentrated; (9) one's facial complexion is serene; (10) one dies unconfused; and (11) if one does not penetrate further, one fares on to the brahma world."

"When, bhikkhus, the liberation of the mind by loving- kindness has been repeatedly pursued, developed, and cultivated, made a vehicle and basis, carried out, consolidated, and properly undertaken, these eleven benefits are to be expected[45]."

- AN 11.15 (Mettānisamsa Sutta)

In summary, as Karanīya Mettā-Sutta details by avoiding unskilful conduct by body, speech, or thought, and by avoiding ill will (ill will is removed at the third stage of enlightenment, Anagami) and cultivating compassion towards all beings upon gaining the right view (right view is gained at the first stage of enlightenment, i.e. Sotapanna) one will not be reborn, and one will attain full enlightenment by becoming an Arahant. Essentially, upon attaining enlightenment, one develops confidence in the Buddha, Dhamma, and Sangha and an individual comes to realize through direct knowledge that Buddha is the worthy One, the Perfect Sambuddha, the one who understands the world and the teacher of Gods and men. Similarly, noble people come to realize through direct knowledge that the Dhamma has been well-

---

[45] Bhikkhu Bodhi (2012), AN 11.15, *Loving-kindness*, p.1573-1574.

proclaimed by the Buddha. The Sangha who are the disciples of Buddha (as in the Triple Gem) means the noble people who have experienced enlightenment and are freed from self-view, doubts about Buddha and his teachings and are practicing Dhamma in the correct way.

CHAPTER NINE:
DHAMMA AND NON-DHAMMA

Enlightenment is typically achieved through four stages and essentially, the first stage of enlightenment is usually achieved by gaining the right view and right view is achieved by hearing true dhamma from a noble person who has gained the right view of Buddha's teaching. The right view is essential to attain enlightenment. Having the right vision and practicing in line with true Dhamma are contributory factors for attaining enlightenment. Altered versions of teaching that are built upon incorrect views and that claim to be Buddha's teachings lead to confused Dhamma (rather non-Dhamma). The wrong understanding of Dhamma prevents Nibbana or liberation for those who aspire for it.

By hearing Dhamma as proclaimed by Buddha from a noble disciple, if one practices Dhamma diligently and in the correct way, one should be able to attain enlightenment (irrespective of whether one lives in a monastery, forest, or in a house etc.). Although it's been rare, it is now possible to hear Dhamma from noble people and this may be of particular interest to those who are aspiring to attain Nibbana.

Noble disciples are the ones who have attained enlightenment and they are four types (those who have attained Sotapanna, Sakadagami, Anagami and Arahant). All Arahants have the same understanding of Dhamma and will teach the same Dhamma. By understanding true Dhamma leading to Nibbana or liberation, one can eliminate all stress and sufferings if one aspires for it. A passage of the Tatiyaadhamma Sutta summarises as:

"Bhikkhus, what is non-Dhamma and what is the Dhamma should be understood, and what is harmful and what is beneficial should also be understood. Having understood what is non-Dhamma and what is the

Dhamma, and also what is harmful and what is beneficial, one should practice in accordance with the Dhamma and with what is beneficial."

"Wrong view is non-Dhamma; right view is the Dhamma. The numerous bad unwholesome qualities that originate with wrong view as condition: these are harmful. The numerous wholesome qualities that reach fulfillment by development with right view as condition: these are beneficial[46]."

-AN 10. 173 (Tatiyaadhamma Sutta)

See the following quotation, a passage of the Saddhammappatirūpaka Sutta which explains that there will be fewer enlightened people when the true teaching of Buddha is disappearing:

"When sentient beings are in decline and the true teaching is disappearing there are more training rules and fewer enlightened mendicants."

"The true teaching doesn't disappear as long the counterfeit of the true teaching hasn't appeared in the world. But when the counterfeit of the true teaching appears in the world then the true teaching disappears[47]."

- SN 16.13 (Saddhammappatirūpaka Sutta)

This indicates that it is important to preserve and appreciate the Buddha's true teaching so that people will be able to attain enlightenment. One must cultivate certain qualities to practice Dhamma in the right way, and a passage of the Sammādiṭṭhi Sutta summarises as:

"Bhikkhus, a bhikkhu who possesses four qualities is practicing the unmistakable way and has laid the groundwork for the destruction of the taints. What four? The thought of renunciation, the thought of good will, the thought of non-harming, and right view. A bhikkhu who

---

[46] Bhikkhu Bodhi (2012), AN10.173, *Non-Dhamma*, p.1516.
[47] Ref: Saddhammappatirūpakasutta: With Kassapa, SN 16.13, Linked Discourses with Kassapa, translated by Pali from Bhikku Sujato (2021), SuttaCentral. Retrieved from: https://suttacentral.net/sn16.13/en/sujato

possesses these four qualities is practicing the unmistakable way and has laid the ground work for the destruction of the taints[48]."

- AN 4. 72 (Sammādiṭṭhi Sutta)

---

[48] Ref: Bhikkhu Bodhi (2012), AN 4.72(2) *View*, p.460.

CHAPTER TEN:
RIGHT VIEW

The noble eightfold path leading to enlightenment begins with the right view. Right view through direct knowledge comes to establish when one attains Sothapanna and when that happens, at once, three fetters are eliminated (self-view, doubts about Buddha, Dhamma and noble sangha, and attachments for rites and rituals).

The purpose of the right view is to gain an understanding of what Buddha has said and to clear misunderstandings. Right view is the first step of the noble eightfold path. A passage of the Mahā Cattārīsaka Sutta summarises as:

"Therein, bhikkhus, right view comes first. And how does right view come first? One understands wrong view as wrong view and right view as right view: this is one's right view.

"And what, bhikkhus, is wrong view? There is nothing given, nothing offered, nothing sacrificed; no fruit or result of good and bad actions; no this world, no other world; no mother, no father; no beings who are reborn spontaneously; no good and virtuous recluses and brahmins in the world who have realised for themselves by direct knowledge and declare this world and the other world. This is wrong view.

"And what, bhikkhus, is right view? Right view, I say, is twofold: there is right view that is affected by taints, partaking of merit, ripening on the side of attachment and there is right view that is noble, taintless, supramundane, a factor of the path.

"And what, bhikkhus, is right view that is affected by the taints, partaking of merit, ripening on the side of attachment? There is what is given and what is offered and what is sacrificed; there is fruit and result of good and bad actions; there is this world and the other world; there is mother and father; there are beings who are reborn spontaneously; there are in the world good and virtuous recluses and brahmins who have realised for themselves by direct knowledge and declare this world and the other world. This is right view affected by taints, partaking of merit, ripening on the side of attachment.

"And what, bhikkhus, is right view that is noble, taintless, supramundane, a factor of the path? The wisdom, the faculty of wisdom, the power of wisdom, the investigation-of-states enlightenment factor, the path factor of right view in one whose mind is noble, whose mind is taintless, who possesses the noble path and is developing the noble path: this is right view that is noble, taintless, supramundane, a factor of the path.

"One makes an effort to abandon wrong view and to enter upon right view: this is one's right effort. Mindfully one abandons wrong view, mindfully one enters upon and abides in right view: this is one's right mindfulness. Thus these three states run and circle around right view, that is, right view, right effort, and right mindfulness[49]"*

-MN 117 (Mahā Cattārīsaka Sutta)

Listening to the true Dhamma and appropriate attention are factors for stream-entry. The Ghosa Suttas summarises as:

"Bhikkhus, there are these two conditions for the arising of wrong view. What two? The utterance of another [person] and careless attention. These are the two conditions for the arising of wrong view".

---

[49] Ref: Bhikkhu Bodhi (1995), The Middle Length Discourses of the Buddha, A New Translation of the Majjima Nikaya, MN 117, *The Great Forty* p.934-935. *(View: 4, 5, 6, 7, 8 and 9)

"Bhikkhus, there are these two conditions for the arising of right view. What two? The utterance of another [person] and careful attention. These are the two conditions for the arising of right view[50]."*

-AN 2.125-126 (Ghosa Suttas)

In essence, one must gain the right view to practice the noble eightfold path in the correct way to attain enlightenment. A passage of the Micchatta Sutta summarises as:

"In dependence on the right course, there is success, not failure. And how is it that in dependence on the right course, there is success, not failure? (1) "For one of right view, (2) right intention originates. For one of right intention, right speech originates. For one of right speech, (4) right action originates. For one of right action, (5) right livelihood originates. For one of right livelihood, (6) right effort originates. For one of right effort, (7) right mindfulness originates. For one of right mindfulness, (8) right concentration originates. For one of right concentration, (9) right knowledge originates. For one of right knowledge, (10) right liberation originates. In this way, in dependence on the right course, there is success, not failure.[51]"

- AN 10.103 (Micchatta Sutta)

Right view develops from the practice of reflecting on non-self-view in daily life. A passage of the Isidatta Sutta summarises as:

"And, venerable sir, how does self-identity view not come into being?"

"There is the case, householder, where a well-instructed disciple of the noble ones—who has regard for noble ones, is well-versed & disciplined in their Dhamma; who has regard for people of integrity, is well-versed & disciplined in their Dhamma—doesn't assume form to be the self, or the self as possessing form, or form as in the self, or the self as in form. He doesn't assume feeling to be the self... He doesn't

---

[50] Ref: Bhikkhu Bodhi (2012), AN 2.125(8) and AN 2.126(9), *XI. Desires*, p.178.
[51] Ref: Bhikkhu Bodhi (2012), AN 10.103, *The Wrong Course*, p.1484.

assume perception to be the self... He doesn't assume fabrications to be the self...

He doesn't assume consciousness to be the self, or the self as possessing consciousness, or consciousness as in the self, or the self as in consciousness. This is how self-identity view does not come into being[52]."

- SN 41.3 (Isidatta Sutta)

Typically, after one becomes a Sotapanna, by understanding what Buddha said by realizing it through direct knowledge, it is possible to succeed into the next stages of enlightenment or attain full enlightenment.

---

[52] Ref: "Isidatta Sutta: About Isidatta", SN 41.3, Translated from Pali by Thanissaro Bhikkhu (1998), dhammatalks.org. Retrieved from: https://www.dhammatalks.org/suttas/SN/SN41_3.html

CHAPTER ELEVEN:
SUPPORTIVE FACTORS FOR ENLIGHTENMENT

There are internal and external factors that contribute to enlightenment and those who listen to Dhamma from noble people (or people who are enlightened) and practice in line with the original Buddha's teachings will be able to attain enlightenment. This is because without insight knowledge one would not be able to attain enlightenment, and those who have gained penetrated knowledge can share their direct knowledge and experience with others.

The Buddha's teachings to be reflected and practiced in daily life and one who wants to attain enlightenment should try and cultivate wholesome qualities and avoid unwholesome qualities in all awakening states. A passage of the Paṭhama Sekha Sutta summarises as:

"Monks, with regard to internal factors, I do not see another single factor so helpful as wise consideration for a monk who is a trainee, who has not yet attained liberation, but lives aspiring for the supreme security from bondage, Nibbāna. Monks, a monk who reflects according to the Dhamma abandons what is unwholesome and develops what is wholesome[53]".

- Itv 16 (Paṭhama Sekha Sutta)

A passage of the Dutiya Sekha Sutta summarises as:

"Monks, with regard to external factors, I do not see another single factor so helpful as noble friendship for a monk who is a trainee, who

---

[53] Ref: "Paṭhama Sekha Sutta: The Trainee", Itv 16, Itivuttaka, Kiribathgoda Ganananda Thero (2017), Suttafriends.org. Retrieved from: https://suttafriends.org/sutta/itv16/

has not yet attained liberation but lives aspiring for the supreme security from bondage, Nibbāna. Monks, a monk who has noble friends abandons what is unwholesome and develops what is wholesome[54]"

-Itv 17 (Dutiya Sekha Sutta)

When all supportive factors are in place, it becomes possible for an individual to attain enlightenment. See the following quotation, a passage of the Therīgāthā which record the experience of an Arahant Nun as:

"I am not lazy or arrogant. I possess a virtuous life and practice the Buddha's training. So why am I not able to achieve Nibbāna?

"I poured water on my feet to wash them. I saw that water flow down from high to low.

"I concentrated my mind very well on that incident. My mind became tamed like the best type of horse. Then I took the lamp and entered my hut.

"With the light of the lamp I found the bed and sat on it. To put out the flame, I pulled down the wick of the oil lamp. That was the moment my mind was liberated from all defilements, just like the extinguishing of an oil lamp[55]."

- The Verses of Arahant Nun Paṭācārā (Thig 5.10)

A passage of the Vipallāsasutta summarises as:

"...But when the Buddhas arise in the world, shedding radiance, they shine a light on this teaching, that leads to the tilling of suffering.

---

[54] Ref: "Dutiya Sekha Sutta, The Noble Friend", Itv 17, Itivuttaka, Kiribathgoda Ganananda Thero (2017), Suttafriends.org. Retrieved from: https://suttafriends.org/sutta/itv17/

[55] Ref: The Verses of Arahant Nun Paṭācārā (Verses 113, 114, 115, 116), Thig 5.10, Therīgāthā, Kiribathgoda Ganananda Thero (2017), Suttafriends.org. Retrieved from: https://suttafriends.org/sutta/thig5-10/

When a wise person hears them, they get their mind back. Seeing impermanence as impermanence, suffering as suffering, not-self as not-self, and ugliness as ugliness—taking up right view, they've risen above all suffering[56]."

- AN 4.49 (Vipallāsasutta)

---

[56] Ref: "Vipallāsasutta: Perversions", AN 4:49, Bhikkhu Sujato (2017), Retrieved from: https://suttacentral.net/an4.49/en/sujato

CHAPTER TWELVE:
Sensual Desires

In essence, one could argue that most beings are attracted to sensual pleasures. The loss of sensual pleasures can bring sorrow and disappointment to those who desire them. For those who wish to reduce and eliminate mental sufferings, it will be beneficial to train the mind to deal with unfulfilled expectations by awakening the mind to gain an accurate understanding of reality to avoid the mental sufferings that come with unfulfilled expectations.

At the first stage of enlightenment, one eliminates self-view and along with the removal of self-view, stress, and suffering cease to a greater extent. Realistically, one cannot satisfy all desires at all times. Realizing this, one can eliminate the unwanted stress that comes due to unfulfilled desires and train one's mind to accept that it is normal to experience unfulfilled expectations in life. At the third stage of enlightenment, one eliminates sensual desires and ill will at the same time. This happens naturally during the process of enlightenment, when one gains the insight of non-self-view that drives one towards the higher stages of enlightenment naturally due to insight. Therefore, one who aspire to achieve enlightenment requires to eliminate self-view first. A passage of Theragāthā records as:

"Those days I followed a wrong thinking pattern. I was addicted to decorating my body. My mind was not peaceful because it was filled with obsession and sensual lust. I was conceited."

"But the Supreme Buddha, the kinsman of the sun, is very strategic. With the help of the Buddha, I started to wisely investigate the truth."

"I was firm in the practice. My mind was drowning in existence: I pulled it out. I lifted my mind up towards Nibbāna[57]".

- The Verses of Arahant Nanda (Thag 2.19)

A passage of the Dhammapada summarises as:

"Khemaka, in addition to being rich, was also very good-looking and women were very much attracted to him. They could hardly resist him and naturally fell a prey to him. Khemaka committed adultery without compunction. The king's men caught him three times for sexual misconduct and brought him to the presence of the king. But King Pasenadi of Kosala did not take action because Khemaka was the nephew of Anathapindika. So Anathapindika himself took his nephew to the Buddha. The Buddha talked to Khemaka about the depravity of sexual misconduct and the seriousness of the consequences..

Verse 309: Four misfortunes befall a man who is unmindful of right conduct and commit sexual misconduct with another man's wife: acquisition of demerit, disturbed sleep, reproach, and suffering in niraya.

At the end of the discourse Khemaka attained Sotapatti Fruition[58]".

- Dhammapada Verses 309

A passage of Theragāthā summarises as:

"Those peacocks' necks are blue. They have beautiful tail feathers. Their beaks are also beautiful. They sing beautiful songs. This great earth is well covered in grass. The blue flowing water is very beautiful. The clouds in this sky are also very beautiful."

"The life of one with a beautiful mind is also like this. Therefore, meditate. How wonderful is it to be liberated from defilements based upon

---

[57] Ref: The Verses of Arahant Nanda, Thag 2.19, Theragāthā, Thag 2, Kiribathgoda Ganananda Thero (2017), Suttafriends.org. Retrieved from: https://suttafriends.org/sutta/thag2-1/
[58] Ref: Daw Mya Tin, (1986), The Dhammapada: Verses and Stories.

the Buddha's path? One should experience the most pure, subtle, and very hard to see Nibbāna[59]".

- The Verses of Arahant Cūḷaka, (Thag 2.46)

At the preliminary stage in the path to enlightenment, it is beneficial to lay a foundation of moral disciplines as the moral discipline will lead to concentration which will allow one to investigate true Dhamma (and to develop wisdom). To attain the first stage of enlightenment, one must maintain precepts or training rules and at the same time, one must meditate on the qualities of Buddha and non-self-view. Upon attaining the first stage of enlightenment, one will naturally behave with morals due to insight without needing to observe precepts as rules. For those who aspire to attain enlightenment, as a form of training, it will be beneficial to reflect on non-self-view in daily life and the qualities of Buddha, Dhamma, and noble Sangha to eliminate the first three fetters and to gain the non-self-view through insight. Upon attaining the first stage of enlightenment, one must meditate on the foulness of the body to eliminate sensual desires, and the right practice will lead to the fruition of the attainment of the Anagami state. To attain Arahathship, one would benefit from reflecting on the non-permanent nature of thoughts and consciousness as a form of meditation to eliminate upper fetters.

---

[59] Ref: The The Verses of Arahant Cūḷaka, Thag 2.46, Theragāthā, Thag 2, Kiribathgoda Gananananda Thero (2017), Suttafriends.org. Retrieved from: https://suttafriends.org/sutta/thag2-1/

CHAPTER THIRTEEN:
THE FOUR NOBLE TRUTHS AND LIFE EXPERIENCES

There are four Noble Truths, and they are the basic formulation of Buddha's teachings. They are:

1. Presence of suffering in life: Buddha's insight was that our lives are a struggle and that finding ultimate satisfaction in any existence is not achievable because everything is subject to change.

2. The cause of suffering (or dukkha) is the root of self-view experienced in the mind itself.

3. The cessation of suffering comes with the cessation of craving, when we eliminate the self-view, the suffering that occurs in the mind due to self-view will be eliminated.

4. There is a path that leads from suffering, there is a unified path one can follow to train oneself in eliminating non-self-view and to withdraw all fetters and that is by gaining the right view and to follow the Noble Eightfold path that comes with the right view which is the forerunner of Noble Eightfold path.

The first noble truth is often realized when one experiences real-life difficulties. Many examples can be found across the Pali Canon as evident on this matter. Below are a few illustrative examples, a few passages of the Therīgāthā and Theragāthā summarise as:

"My life was miserable. I witnessed the death of my two sons and my husband. I saw the funeral pyre on which the bodies of my mother, father and sister were being burnt. I have cut out the dart of sorrow."

"I have lowered the heavy load of defilements. What had to be done to end suffering has been done. These were said by the enlightened Nun Kisāgotamī, who has a fully liberated mind[60]".

- Verses were said by Arahant Nun Kisāgotamī (Thig 10.1)

"I couldn't bear the pain of my son's death. I went crazy and lost my mindfulness. I didn't even wear clothes. With a messy head of hair, I wandered here and there."

"I lived on heaps of rubbish in the streets, in cemeteries, and on highways. I wandered like this for three years, suffering from hunger and thirst."

"One day, I saw the Supreme Buddha entering the city of Mithilā. I saw the Supremely Enlightened Buddha, the tamer of the untamed beings and the one who has no fear at all."

"With that sight, I regained my mind and came to my senses. I went to the Buddha and worshiped him. Gautama Supreme Buddha showed pity on me and preached the Dhamma to me."

"Having heard the excellent Dhamma, I became a nun. Following the Supreme Teacher's instruction, I attained the bliss of Nibbāna[61]."

- The Verses of Arahant Nun Vāseṭṭhi (Thig 6.2)

---

[60]Ref: The Verses of Arahant Nun Kisāgotamī, Thig 10.1, Therīgāthā,, Kiribathgoda Ganananda Thero(2017), Suttafriends.org. Retrieved from: https://suttafriends.org/sutta/thig10-1/
*Noble people are the individuals who have attained enlightenment through four stages (Sotapanna, Sakadagami, Anagami, and Arahant) and are able to share their direct knowledge of Dhamma gained through personal experience with others.
[61] Ref: The Verses of Arahant Nun Vāseṭṭhi, Thig 6.2, Therīgāthā, Kiribathgoda Ganananda Thero (2017), Suttafriends.org. Retrieved from: https://suttafriends.org/sutta/thig6-2/

A passage of the verses of Arahant nun Gaṅgātīrya record as:

"I live on the bank of the Ganges River. There my hut is made out of three palm leaves. My bowl is like a funeral pot which is used to sprinkle water on dead bodies. I wear rag robes."

"For two years I only spoke one word. In the third year after I became a monk, I split and destroyed the darkness of ignorance[62]."

- The Verses of Arahant Gaṅgātīrya (Thag 2.4)

When the life experience becomes unpleasant, as a way of escape from unpleasant life situations or experiences, one comes to seek and appreciate the enlightenment. The truth of the cause of suffering is self-view or in other words, thinking that everything bad happens to self leads to distress. On the contrary, thinking that everything bad happens to non-self leads to eradicate stress, and for one who can practice this in life, it will become possible to experience peace and also to gain the right view. As a form of practice, if one could try and relax when meet with stressful situations in life to bring back mindfulness to reflect on non-self-view for a few minutes and extend such reflective time to build up insight, this would help one train the mind to establish non-self-view more permanently over time. By following Buddha's teaching as proclaimed by him, one can attain enlightenment to end stress and suffering.

---

[62] Ref: These verses were said by Arahant Gaṅgātīrya, Thag 2.4, Theragāthā, Kiribathgoda Ganananda Thero (2017), Suttafriends.org. Retrieved from: https://suttafriends.org/sutta/thag2-1/

CHAPTER FOURTEEN:
EVERYDAY LIFE AND DHAMMA

The teachings of Buddha are open to individuals who have imperfections in their conduct. By eliminating impurity in mind and conduct, one can experience peace and happiness within. This chapter discusses some of the inspiring stories and backgrounds of noble people. These stories seem to suggest that bad experiences in life can turn into an achievement of enlightenment and the realization of Nibbana eliminates suffering.

The selected passages of the Therīgāthā and the Theragāthā record as:

"I used this life full of pain only for practicing the Dhamma diligently. Craving has been destroyed. I have attained Nibbāna and completed the Buddha's training"[63].

    - The verses of Arahant Nun Abhayā (Thig 2.9)

"I used to lead a very strange life. I pulled out my hair with my hand. I didn't brush my teeth. I wore only one piece of cloth. Back then I thought that wrong deeds were correct deeds and correct deeds were wrong deeds.

"One day I saw the stainless Buddha surrounded by a community of monks climbing down from the Mount Gijjhakūṭa in the evening. I went to the presence of the Supreme Buddha.

---

[63] Ref: The Verses of Arahant Nun Abhayā, Thig 2.9, Therīgāthā, Kiribathgoda Ganananda Thero (2017), Suttafriends.org. Retrieved from: https://suttafriends.org/sutta/thig2-1/

"Kneeling down and placing my hands together, I worshiped the Great Buddha. The Buddha said to me: "Come here Bhaddā." That was my higher ordination[64]."

- The Verses of Arahant Nun Bhaddā Kuṇḍalakesā
(Thig 5.9)

A passage of the Kimsila Sutta summarises as:

"While those who delight in the Dhamma taught by the noble ones, are unsurpassed in word, action, & mind. They, established in calm, composure, & concentration, have reached what discernment & learning have as their heartwood[65]".

-SN 2.9 (Kimsila Sutta)

A passage of the Therīgāthā summarises as:

"In the past, I was extremely beautiful and fit. I was intoxicated by all the luxurious comforts around me. I was self-absorbed and conceited. I despised other women.

"Back then I decorated my body with beautiful ornaments. Having dressed in a way that foolish people praise, I would wait at the corner of the street like a deer hunter having placed a trap.

"I used to wear seductive clothing. I did various sorts of tricks to attract men. Foolish men fell easily under my spell, and I lured them towards me."

"I have cut off all ties that lead to rebirth as a human or a god.

---

[64] Ref: The Verses of Arahant Nun Bhaddā Kuṇḍalakesā, Thig 5.9, Therīgāthā, Kiribathgoda Ganananda Thero (2017), Suttafriends.org. Retrieved from: https://suttafriends.org/sutta/thig5-9/
[65] Ref: "Kimsila Sutta: With What Virtue?", SN 2.9, KN, Traslated by Thanissaro Bhikkhu, dhammatalks.org, Retrieved from: https://www.dhammatalks.org/suttas/KN/StNp/StNp2_9.html

I have destroyed all taints. I have become cool and quenched[66]."

- The verses of Arahant Nun Vimalā (Thig 5.2)

A passage of the Theragāthā summarises as:

"Seeking purity in the wrong way, I was offering fire sacrifices in the forest. Not knowing the path to Nibbāna, I practiced various austerities. But they did not benefit me in any way."

"But see the excellence of the Dhamma! I achieved the Supreme bliss of Nibbāna through a happy path. I achieved the Triple Knowledge, the Buddha's path has been fully followed by me[67]."

- The Verses of Arahant Aggikabhāradvāja (Thag 3.1)

The Story from the Dhammapada Verse 216 (Annatarabrahmana Vatthu) summarises as:

"The brahmin lived in Savatthi, and he was a non-Buddhist. But the Buddha knew that the brahmin would attain Sotapatti Fruition in the near future. So the Buddha went to where the brahmin was ploughing his field and talked to him. The brahmin became friendly and was thankful to the Buddha for taking an interest in him and his work in the field. One day, he said to the Buddha, "Samana Gotama, when I have gathered my rice from this field, I will first offer you some before I take it. I will not eat my rice until I have given you some." However, the Buddha knew beforehand that the brahmin would not have the opportunity to harvest the rice from his field that year, but he kept silent.

---

[66] Ref: These verses were said by Arahant Nun Vimalā, Thig 5.2, Therīgāthā, Kiribathgoda Gananada Thero (2017), Suttafriends.org. Retrieved from: https://suttafriends.org/sutta/thig5-2/

[67] Ref: The Verses of Arahant Aggikabhāradvāja, Thag 3.1, Theragāthā, Kiribathgoda Gananada Thero (2017), Suttafriends.org. Retrieved from: https://suttafriends.org/sutta/thag3-1/

Then, on the night before the brahmin was to harvest his rice, there was a heavy downpour of rain which washed away the entire crop of rice. The brahmin was very much distressed, because he would no longer be able to offer any rice to his friend, the Samana Gotama.

The Buddha went to the house of the brahmin and the brahmin talked to him about the great disaster that had befallen him. In reply, the Buddha said, *"Brahmin, you do not know the cause of sorrow, but I know. If sorrow and fear arise, they arise because of craving."*

Then the Buddha spoke in verse as follows:

Verse 216: Craving begets sorrow, craving begets fear. For him who is free from craving there is no sorrow; how can there be fear for him?

- Dhammapada Verse 216

At the end of the discourse the brahmin attained Sotapatti Fruition."[68]

See the following quotation which described the experience of an enlightened monk, a passage of the Theragāthā records as:

"For fifty-five years, I didn't wear anything at all. I covered my body with dust. I only ate one meal a month, putting a very small quantity of rice on my tongue. I ripped out my beard and hair."

"I rejected seats; I stood on one leg. I ate dry dung and I did not accept any invitations."

"In this way, I collected a lot of demerit leading to a bad destination. While I was drowning in the great flood of defilements. I was able to go for refuge to the Supreme Buddha."

---

[68] Ref: Daw Mya Tin, (1986), The Dhammapada: Verses and Stories.

"See the assurance of my arrival to the Noble Triple Gem! See the excellence of the Dhamma! I achieved the Triple Knowledge. The Buddha's path has been fully followed by me[69]."

- Arahant Jambuka (Thag 4.5)

See the quotations below, the passages of the Theragāthā record as:

"That day, my former wife, decorated with jewelry and ornaments, surrounded by servant girls, came up to me carrying her son upon her hip."

"When I saw my son's mother decorated with ornaments, well dressed, coming to me, she seemed to me like a snare put by Māra."

"Based on this incident, wise consideration arose in me. The danger of sensual pleasures was clear to me. Disenchantment with life was established in my mind."

"Based on this same incident, my mind was liberated from all defilements. See the excellence of this Dhamma! I too attained the Triple Knowledge. The Buddha's path has been fully followed by me[70]."

-Arahant Candana, (Thag 4.9)

During Buddha's time, many people attained enlightenment by hearing a single Dhamma talk from Buddha or a noble disciple. One who practices Dhamma in the correct way by understanding Buddha's teachings should be able to attain enlightenment. A passage of the Theragāthā record as:

---

[69] Ref: The Verses of Arahant Jambuka, Theragāthā, Thag 4.5, Theragāthā, Kiribathgoda Ganananda Thero (2017), Suttafriends.org. Retrieved from: https://suttafriends.org/sutta/thag4-5/
[70] Ref: The Verses of Arahant Candana, Theragāthā, Thag 4.9, Theragāthā, Kiribathgoda Ganananda Thero (2017), Suttafriends.org. Retrieved from: https://suttafriends.org/sutta/thag4-9/

"When Dhamma is well practiced, it brings happiness. The benefit of practising the Dhamma well is this: the one who practises the Dhamma doesn't go to a bad destination."

"Dhamma practise and wrong practise don't have equal results. Wrong practice takes beings to hell. Dhamma practice takes beings to heaven."

"Therefore, one should desire the Good Dhamma. One should rejoice in the Dhamma of the founder of the Great Path, the one with an unshaken mind. The wise disciples with the best refuge, who stand in the Dhamma of the best teacher, can reach Nibbāna.[71]"

- The Verses of Arahant Dhammika, (Thag 4.10)

The Buddha's teachings allow an individual to abandon the causes of suffering. For those who wish to proceed to the enlightenment path, it will be helpful to practice reflecting on non-self-view in daily life, particularly when encountering stressful real-life situations. Similarly, it is important that one goes to refuge in Buddha, his teachings and Sangha (noble disciples of Buddha) and in doing so, to reflect the qualities of Triple Gem daily (and in all awakening states) as this is the mind of an Arahant, and along the same time to reflect on non-self-view.

---

[71] Ref: The Verses of Arahant Dhammika, Theragāthā, Thag 4.10, Theragāthā, Kiribathgoda Ganananda Thero (2017), Suttafriends.org. Retrieved from: https://suttafriends.org/sutta/thag4-10/

CHAPTER FIFTEEN:
TEN FETTERS AND ABANDONING THE FETTERS

Four stages of Nibbāna (Nirvana) are Sotapanna, Sakadagami, Anagami, and Arahant. Upon attaining the first stage of enlightenment (Sotapanna) and thereby eliminating three fetters, an individual experiences joy and contentment knowing that all stressful things that happen in life are not happening to self through direct knowledge.

There are ten fetters that one eliminates during the stages of enlightenment. The Saṁyojanasutta records as:

"Mendicants, there are ten fetters. What ten? The five lower fetters and the five higher fetters. What are the five lower fetters? Identity view, doubt, misapprehension of precepts and observances, sensual desire, and ill will. These are the five lower fetters.

What are the five higher fetters? Desire for rebirth in the realm of luminous form, desire for rebirth in the formless realm, conceit, restlessness, and ignorance. These are the five higher fetters. These are the ten fetters[72]."

— AN 10.13 (Saṁyojanasutta)

Fetters are eliminated naturally during the process of enlightenment due to insight of non-self-view gained at the first stage of enlightenment (i.e. Sotapanna) and thus, and it is worth putting efforts to attain the stage of the first stage of enlightenment (i.e Sotapanna) as the rest of the enlightenment stages will naturally follow through in due

---

[72] Ref: "Saṁyojanasutta: Fetters", AN 10.13, Translated from Pali by Bhikkhu Sujato (2017), Suttacentral.net. Retrieved from: https://suttacentral.net/an10.13/en/sujato

course at the right time. Reflecting the qualities of Buddha, his teachings and his noble disciples (meditating on the qualities of Triple Gem) will be the kind of useful training for those who want to train to attain the first stage of enlightenment, and please see below the quotation taken from Paṭhamamahānāmasutta as evident for this matter:

"Sir, I have heard that several mendicants are making a robe for the Buddha, thinking that when his robe was finished and the three months of the rains residence had passed the Buddha would set out wandering. Now, we spend our life in various ways. Which of these should we practice?"

"Good, good, Mahānāma! It's appropriate that gentlemen such as you come to me and ask: We spend our life in various ways. Which of these should we practice?' The faithful succeed, not the faithless. The energetic succeed, not the lazy. The mindful succeed, not the unmindful. Those with immersion succeed, not those without immersion. The wise succeed, not the witless. When you're grounded on these five things, go on to develop six further things.

"Firstly, you should recollect the Realized One: 'That Blessed One is perfected, a fully awakened Buddha, accomplished in knowledge and conduct, holy, knower of the world, supreme guide for those who wish to train, teacher of gods and humans, awakened, blessed.' When a noble disciple recollects the Realized One their mind is not full of greed, hate, and delusion. At that time their mind is unswerving, based on the Realized One. A noble disciple whose mind is unswerving finds joy in the meaning and the teaching, and finds joy connected with the teaching. When they're joyful, rapture springs up. When the mind is full of rapture, the body becomes tranquil. When the body is tranquil, they feel bliss. And when they're blissful, the mind becomes immersed in samādhi. This is called a noble disciple who lives in balance among people who are unbalanced, and lives untroubled among people who are troubled. They've entered the stream of the teaching and developed the recollection of the Buddha.

"Furthermore, you should recollect the teaching: 'The teaching is well explained by the Buddha—visible in this very life, immediately effective, inviting inspection, relevant, so that sensible people can know it for themselves.' When a noble disciple recollects the teaching their mind is not full of greed, hate, and delusion... This is called a noble disciple who lives in balance among people who are unbalanced, and lives untroubled among people who are troubled. They've entered the stream of the teaching and developed the recollection of the teaching.

"Furthermore, you should recollect the Saṅgha: 'The Saṅgha of the Buddha's disciples is practicing the way that's good, direct, methodical, and proper. It consists of the four pairs, the eight individuals. This is the Saṅgha of the Buddha's disciples that is worthy of offerings dedicated to the gods, worthy of hospitality, worthy of a religious donation, worthy of greeting with joined palms, and is the supreme field of merit for the world.' When a noble disciple recollects the Saṅgha their mind is not full of greed, hate, and delusion... This is called a noble disciple who lives in balance among people who are unbalanced, and lives untroubled among people who are troubled. They've entered the stream of the teaching and developed the recollection of the Saṅgha.

"Furthermore, a noble disciple recollects their own ethical conduct, which is unbroken, impeccable, spotless, and unmarred, liberating, praised by sensible people, not mistaken, and leading to immersion. When a noble disciple recollects their ethical conduct their mind is not full of greed, hate, and delusion. ... This is called a noble disciple who lives in balance among people who are unbalanced, and lives untroubled among people who are troubled. They've entered the stream of the teaching and developed the recollection of their ethical conduct[73]."

- AN 11.11 (Paṭhamamahānāmasutta)

Understanding non-self-view can bring relief to those who can reflect on non-self-view particularly when they encounter stressful real-life situations. By understanding non-self-view through direct knowledge, a noble person eliminates all stress. Upon attaining enlightenment, one develops confidence in the Buddha, Dhamma, and noble Sangha through direct knowledge.

---

[73] Ref: "Paṭhamamahānāmasutta: With Mahānāma (1st)", AN 11.11, The First Fifty-Five, Translated by Bhikkhu Sujato (2018), Suttacentral.net. Retrieved from: https://suttacentral.net/an11.11/en/sujato

At the same time, a noble person develops other good qualities such as gentleness, humbleness, courteousness, and responsibility towards others (that would mean becoming a good parent towards children, becoming a good child towards parents, becoming a good sibling, a good employee and so on).

Most of these qualities can be found in the famous Karaṇīya Mettā-Sutta that provides a guideline on how one can practice attaining Nibbana or peace within and similar guidelines can be found in several other Suttas including Mangala Sutta.

In summary, by avoiding unskilful conduct by body, speech, or thought, and by avoiding ill will (ill will is removed at the third stage of enlightenment, Anagami) and cultivating compassion towards all beings upon gaining the right view (right view is gained at the first stage of enlightenment, i.e. Sotapanna) one will not be reborn or will attain full enlightenment by becoming an Arahanth. This may be of interest to those who aspire to achieve enlightenment to know that it is possible to hear Dhamma from noble persons in present times. By practicing Dhamma as proclaimed by Buddha will help one attain enlightenment.

CHAPTER SIXTEEN:
RIGHT VIEW AND GOOD DHAMMA

For those who are interested in achieving enlightenment, (and for Dhamma followers and faithful followers who have the potential to achieve enlightenment), it will be beneficial to follow Buddha's original teachings and avoid third parties. Misinterpreting Dhamma will be an obstacle to the path of enlightenment and understanding what is good Dhamma and bad Dhamma can help one understand Buddha's teachings to achieve results. A passage of the Sādhusutta summarises as:

"And what, bhikkhus, is bad? Wrong view, wrong intention, wrong speech, wrong action, wrong livelihood, wrong effort, wrong mindfulness, wrong concentration, wrong knowledge, and wrong liberation. This is called the bad.

"And what, bhikkhus, is good? Right view, right intention, right speech, right action, right livelihood, right effort, right mindfulness, right concentration, right knowledge, and right liberation. This is called good[74]".

- AN 10.134 (Sādhusutta)

To progress in the path of enlightenment, one must associate with noble people and avoid bad Dhamma. A passage of the Sevitabbasutta summarises as:

"Bhikkhus, one should not associate with a person who possesses ten qualities. What ten? Wrong view, wrong intention, wrong speech, wrong action, wrong livelihood, wrong effort, wrong mindfulness,

---

[74] Ref: Bhikkhu Bodhi (2012), AN 10.134, *Good,* p.1505.

wrong concentration, wrong knowledge, and wrong liberation. One should not associate with a person who possesses these ten qualities.

"Bhikkhus, one should associate with a person who possesses ten qualities. What ten? Right view, right intention, right speech, right action, right livelihood, right effort, right mindfulness, right concentration, right knowledge, and right liberation. One should associate with a person who possesses these ten qualities[75]".

- AN 10.155 (Sevitabbasutta)

Right view is developed at the first stage of enlightenment. To gain right view, one should pay careful attention to Dhamma and practice Dhamma as proclaimed by Buddha.

The selected two verses of the Tayodhamma Sutta summarise as:

"Without having abandoned these, three things, one is incapable of abandoning personal-existence view, doubt, and wrong grasp of behavior and observances. What three? Careless attention, following a wrong path, and mental sluggishness. Without having abandoned these three things, one is incapable of abandoning personal-existence view, doubt, and wrong grasp of behavior and observances[76]".

"Having abandoned these three things, one is capable of abandoning personal-existence view, doubt, and wrong grasp of behavior and observances. What three? Careless attention, following a wrong path, and mental sluggishness. Having abandoned these three things, one is capable of abandoning personal-existence view, doubt, and wrong grasp of behavior and observances[77]".

-AN 10.76 (Tayodhamma sutta)

Those who attain stream-entry experience six rewards, and the selected verses of the Ānisaṁsa Sutta record as:

---

[75] Ref: Bhikkhu Bodhi (2012), AN 10.155, *Associate With (Persons)*, p.1507.
[76] Ref: Bhikkhu Bodhi (2012), AN 10.76, *Three Things*, [3], p.1435.
[77] Ref: Bhikkhu Bodhi (2012), AN 10.76, *Incapable*, [3], p.1437.

"Bhikkhus, there are these six benefits in realizing the fruit of stream-entry. What six? (1) One is fixed in the good Dhamma; (2) one is incapable of decline; (3) one's suffering is delimited; (4) one comes to possess knowledge not shared by others; (5) one has clearly seen causation; (6) one has clearly seen causally arisen phenomena. These are the six benefits in realizing the fruit of stream -entry[78]."

- AN 6:97 (Ānisaṁsa Sutta)

For those who are interested in attaining enlightenment, it will be beneficial to understand what to expect on attaining the stages of enlightenment and also to practice in ways that allow progress in the enlightenment path. Enlightenment is achieved and experienced through four stages (Sotapanna, Sakadagami, Anagami, and Arahant). Although time may vary between individuals, one who attains the first stage of enlightenment is guaranteed to become an Arahanth. Upon attaining enlightenment, an individual will have the best possible mental state, virtuous (values and ethics) and mind filled with compassion in all awakening states. The right view is the forerunner of the noble eightfold path.

An individual gains the right view at the first stage of enlightenment, and three fetters (self-view, doubts about Buddha, Dhamma and Sangha and attachment for rites and rituals) are eliminated at once. Essentially, upon attaining the first stage of enlightenment, one comes to understand who Buddha is and his teachings are, and who Sangha is. That would indicate a person who achieves the stage of Sotappana will understand through direct knowledge that Buddha is the one who understands the world, Dhamma has been well-proclaimed by the Buddha and that noble Sangha means those who have attained enlightenment through four stages and are practicing in the right way.

In terms of training, it will be beneficial to combine the practice of reflecting on non-self-view along with reflecting the qualities of Buddha, Dhamma, and Sangha as a form of meditation to begin with and to integrate such reflections more into daily life.

---

[78] Ref: Bhikkhu Bodhi (2012), AN 6:97, *Benefits*, p.981-982.

CHAPTER SEVENTEEN:
MERITS

Merit (Pali: puñña), refers to wholesome kamma accumulated as a result of wholesome actions of mind, body and speech. Merits contribute to success and gains in present life, future lives and to attain enlightenment.

The concept of "merit" is tied to the teachings on karma. The word Kamma literally means "action" and Kamma is the idea that all actions have consequences. Beings are owners of their kamma.

Buddha defined kamma as one's intention. A morally good and wholesome action has good consequences. A morally bad and unwholesome action has bad consequences. Selected verses of the Culakammavibhanga Sutta summarise as:

"Master Gotama, what is the cause and condition why human beings are seen to be inferior and superior? For people are seen to be short-lived and long-lived, sickly and healthy, ugly and beautiful, uninfluential and influential, poor and wealthy, low-born and high-born, stupid and wise. What is the cause and condition, Master Gotama, why human beings are seen to be inferior and superior?"

"Student, beings are owners of their actions, heirs of their actions; they originate from their actions, are bound to their actions, have their actions as their refuge. It is action that distinguishes beings as inferior and superior." [79]

- MN 135 (Culakammavibhanga Sutta)

---

[79]Ref: Bhikkhu Nanamoli and Bhikkhu Bodhi (Translated from the Pali by Bikku Nanamoli and Edited and Revised by Bhikku Bodhi) (1995), Culakammavibhanga Sutta, MN 135, A New Translation of the Majjima Nikaya, p.1053.

A passage of the Dutiya Kokālika Sutta summarises as:

"He who praises a person deserving criticism, or criticises a person deserving praise, collects lot of demerit with his mouth. Because of that evil deed, he will never find happiness[80].

- SN 6.10 (Dutiya Kokālika Sutta)

Merits are created on three bases:

1. Giving

2. Virtue

3. Mental development

Dedicating merits to others and rejoicing in other's merits are two common practices within Buddhism. Some of the benefits of good kamma are birth in fortunate circumstances, and happiness.

The story associated with Dhammapada Verse 68 records as:

"A florist, named Sumana, had to supply King Bimbisara of Rajagaha with jasmin flowers every morning. One day, as he was going to the king's palace, he saw the Buddha, with a halo of light-rays radiating from him, coming into town for alms-food accompanied by many bhikkhus. Seeing the Buddha in his resplendent glory, the florist Sumana felt a strong desire to offer his flowers to the Buddha. Then and there, he decided that even if the king were to drive him out of the country or to kill him, he would not offer the flowers to the king for that day. Thus, he threw up the flowers to the sides, to the back and over and above the head of the Buddha. The flowers remained hanging in the air; those over the head formed a canopy of flowers and those at the back and the sides formed walls of flowers. These flowers followed the Buddha in this position as he moved on and stopped when

---

[80]Ref: "Dutiya Kokālika Sutta: Brahma Saṁyutta", SN 6.10, Kiribathgoda Gananananda Thero (2017), Suttafriends.org. Retrieved from: https://suttafriends.org/sutta/sn6-10/

the Buddha stopped. As the Buddha proceeded, surrounded by walls of flowers, and a canopy of flowers, with the six-coloured rays radiating from his body, followed by a large entourage, thousands of people inside and outside of Rajagaha came out of their houses to pay obeisance to the Buddha. As for Sumana, his entire body was suffused with delightful satisfaction (Piti).

The wife of the florist Sumana then went to the king and said that she had nothing to do with her husband failing to supply the king with flowers for that day. The king, being a Sotapanna himself, felt quite happy about the flowers. He came out to see the wonderful sight and paid obeisance to the Buddha. The king also took the opportunity to offer alms-food to the Buddha and his disciples. After the meal, the Buddha returned in the Jetavana monastery and the king followed him for some distance. On arrival back at the palace King Bimbisara sent for Sumana and offered him a reward of eight elephants, eight horses, eight male slaves, eight female slaves, eight maidens and eight thousand in cash.

At the Jetavana monastery, the Venerable Ananda asked the Buddha what benefits Sumana would gain by his good deed done on that day. The Buddha answered that Sumana, having given to the Buddha without any consideration for his life, would not be born in any of the four lower worlds (Apaya) for the next one hundred thousand worlds and that eventually he would become a paccekabuddha. After that, as the Buddha entered the Perfumed Hall (Gandhakuti) the flowers dropped off of their own accord.

That night, at the end of the usual discourse, the Buddha spoke in verse as follows:

Verse 68: That deed is well done if one has not to repent for having done it, and if one is delightful and happy with the result of that deed[81]".

- Dhammapada Verse 68

---

[81] Ref: Daw Mya Tin, (1986), The Dhammapada: Verses and Stories.

Merit creation is linked to kamma and by creating good kamma, one will be able to have good treasures in life and a fortunate birth. An action motivated by generosity, loving-kindness and wisdom has good or happy consequences. A passage of the Ubho-attha Sutta summarises as:

"The wise praise diligence in doing deeds of merit, for one who is wise and diligent achieves both kinds of welfare: Welfare in this life and welfare in lives to come. The intelligent one who achieves both kinds of welfare is called a wise person[82]."

- Itv 23, Ubho-attha Sutta

By observing the moral precepts and by engaging in meritorious deeds, one acquires much merit. Merits are needed for gaining success in this life, afterlife, and to attain enlightenment. By practicing Dhamma in line with Buddha's teachings, one can obtain both worldly and spiritual progress (for example, please see Maha Mangala Sutta) and attain enlightenment. Two verses of the Māpuññabhāyi Sutta summarise as:

"The one who wishes one's own long-lasting happiness should develop deeds of merit: giving, a balanced life, a mind of loving-kindness.

Developing the three things that bring about great happiness, the wise person is reborn in an untroubled happy world.[83]"

-Itv 22, Māpuññabhāyi Sutta

In conclusion, wholesome actions produce wholesome effects, and merits are needed for gaining both worldly success and spiritual success, and to attain enlightenment.

---

[82] Ref: "Ubho-attha Sutta:Both Kinds of Welfare", Itv23, Kiribathgoda Ganananda Thero (2017), Suttafriends.org. Retrieved from: https://suttafriends.org/sutta/itv23/
[83] Ref: "Māpuññabhāyi Sutta: Do Not Fear Merit", Itv 22, Itivuttaka, Kiribathgoda Ganananda Thero (2017), Suttafriends.org. Retrieved from: https://suttafriends.org/sutta/itv22/

CHAPTER EIGHTEEN:
LIFE GOES IN CYCLES

Life goes in circles and this is applicable to everyone. Things repetitively happen over and over again in one's life, and stress may come to establish due to repetitive endless tasks. By attaining enlightenment, one can eliminate stress of ordinary ties. A relevant passage of the Udayasutta records as:

"Again and again, they sow the seed; again and again, the lord god sends rain; again and again, farmers plough the field; again and again, grain is produced for the nation.

Again and again, the beggars beg; again and again, the donors give. Again and again, when the donors have given, again and again, they take their place in heaven.

Again and again, dairy farmers milk; again and again, a calf cleaves to its mother; again and again, oppressing and intimidating; that idiot is reborn again and again.

Again and again, you're reborn and die; again and again, you get carried to a charnel ground. But when they've gained the path for no further rebirth, one of vast wisdom is not reborn again and again[84]."

-SN 7.12 (Udayasutta)

The relevant quotations taken from the Theragāthā summarise as:

---

[84] Ref: "Udayasutta: With Udaya" (SN 7.12, Linked Discourses 7), Translated from Pali by Bhikku Sujato, 2018, Retrieved from: https://suttacentral.net/sn7.12/en/sujato

"Truly the life of a monk is hard. Household life is also hard. The Dhamma is profound. Wealth is hard to obtain. Our lives, maintained by whatever is given, are very hard. Therefore, it is fitting to think always of impermanence[85]".

- The Verse of Arahant Jenta (Thag 1.111)

"But the wise person listens to the Supreme Buddha's Dhamma with a joyful mind. He eliminates all the taints. Having realized Nibbāna, he attains the highest peace.[86]"

- The Verse of Arahant Yasadatta (Thag 5.10)

The Dhammapada Verse 354 summarises as:

"The gift of tile Dhamma excels all gifts; the taste of the Dhamma excels all tastes; delight in the Dhamma excels all delights. The eradication of Craving (i.e., attainment of arahatship) overcomes all ills (samsara dukkha[87])".

- Dhammapada Verse 354

---

[85] Ref: Thag 1.111, Thag 1, Theragāthā, Kiribathgoda Ganananda Thero (2017), Retrieved from: https://suttafriends.org/sutta/thag1-1/

[86] Ref: The Verse of Arahant Yasadatta , (Thag 5.10), Theragāthā,Tranlasted from Sinhala version of Kiribathgoda Ganananda Thero (2017), Retrieved from: https://suttafriends.org/sutta/thag5-10/

[87] Ref: Daw Mya Tin, (1986), The Dhammapada: Verses and Stories.

CHAPTER NINETEEN:
DHAMMA PRACTICE AND FRUITION

Perfect confidence in Buddha, his teachings, and noble Sangha comes from gaining the realization of non-self-view at the first stage of enlightenment (i.e Sotapanna). The realization that there is no unchanging permanent self also leads to non-attachment to any rites and rituals. Thus, for one who has attained the right view (non-self-view), three fetters are at once abandoned. To become Arahant, one must eliminate the five lower fetters, and the five upper fetters. By training precisely in line with Buddha's teachings, one can attain enlightenment. A passage of the Theragāthā summarises as:

"One should cut off five. One should abandon five. One should especially develop the five. The monk who has gone beyond the five is called a "flood-crosser[88]."

-The Verse of Arahant Kuṇḍadhāna (Thag 1.15)

The one who associates with noble people and listen to true Dhamma as proclaimed by Buddha are able to comprehends the Four Noble Truths: suffering, the arising of suffering, the cessation of suffering, and the Noble Eightfold Path. Below is a quotation taken from the Kiṁsīla Sutta:

---

[88] Ref: The Verse of Arahant Kuṇḍadhāna, Thag 1.15, Theragāthā, Kiribathgoda Ganananda Thero (2017), Retrieved from: https://suttafriends.org/sutta/thag1-1/

"Delighting in Dharma by Noble Ones taught, their mind, speech and body all unsurpassed—in gentleness, peace, meditative-states firm, attained to the essence of wisdom and learning[89]".

- Snp 2.9 (Kiṁsīla Sutta)

The Noble Sangha or the Sangha of Buddha is formed of four types of persons, who are at four different stages of enlightenment (Sotapanna, Sakadagami, Anagami and Arahant). Listening to true Dhamma from noble people will help one make a progress in the path leading to the stages of Nibbana (Sotapanna, Sakadagami, Anagami, and Arahant). One can attain enlightenment by practicing Dhamma in line with Buddha's teachings.

A passage of the Sīlasampanna Sutta records as:

"Having heard the Buddha's message from the noble ones, the wise, with perfect understanding, realize the end of rebirths and never return to birth[90]."

- Itv 104 (Sīlasampanna Sutta)

At the preliminary stage in the path to enlightenment, it is beneficial to lay a foundation of moral disciplines as the moral discipline will lead to concentration which will allow one to investigate true Dhamma (and to develop wisdom). Upon attaining the first stage of enlightenment, one will naturally behave with morals due to insight without needing to observe precepts as rules. See the following quotation as evident of this matter. A passage of the Ratha-vinīta Sutta summarises as:

"Purity in terms of virtue is simply for the sake of purity in terms of mind. Purity in terms of mind is simply for the sake of purity in terms of view. Purity in terms of view is simply for the sake of purity in

---

[89] Ref: Laurence Khantipalo Mills, "Kiṁsīla Sutta, What is Good Conduct?", Snp 2.9, Sutta Nipāta, Retrieved from: https://a-buddha-ujja.hu/snp-2.9/en/mills
[90] Ref: "Sīlasampanna Sutta: Possessing Virtue", Itv 104, Itivuttaka, Kiribathgoda Gananananda Thero (2017), Suttafriends.org. Retrieved from: https://suttafriends.org/sutta/itv104/

terms of the overcoming of perplexity. Purity in terms of the overcoming of perplexity is simply for the sake of purity in terms of knowledge & vision of what is & is not the path. Purity in terms of knowledge & vision of what is & is not the path is simply for the sake of purity in terms of knowledge & vision of the way. Purity in terms of knowledge & vision of the way is simply for the sake of purity in terms of knowledge & vision. Purity in terms of knowledge & vision is simply for the sake of total unbinding through lack of clinging. And it's for the sake of total unbinding through lack of clinging that the holy life is lived under the Blessed One[91]."

- MN 24 (Ratha-vinīta Sutta)

When Dhamma is practiced correctly, it brings good results. One comes to realize about one's awakening and one comes to experience what's heard or read in the Pali Canon becomes a personnel experience. A passage of the Theragāthā records as:

"Dhamma can truly protect the one who practices it. When Dhamma is well practiced, it brings happiness. The benefit of practising the Dhamma well is this: the one who practises the Dhamma doesn't go to a bad destination."

"Dhamma practise and wrong practise don't have equal results. Wrong practice takes beings to hell. Dhamma practice takes beings to heaven."

"Therefore, one should desire the Good Dhamma. One should rejoice in the Dhamma of the founder of the Great Path, the one with an unshaken mind. The wise disciples with the best refuge, who stand in the Dhamma of the best teacher, can reach Nibbāna[92]."

-Verses Arahant Dhammika (Thag 4.10)

---

[91] Ref: "Ratha-vinīta Sutta: Relay Chariots", MN 24, Translated by Thanissaro Bhikkhu, dhammatalks.org. Retrieved from: https://www.dhammatalks.org/suttas/MN/MN24.html
[92] Ref: Verses Arahant Dhammika, Thag 4.10, Theragāthā, Kiribathgoda Ganananda Thero (2017), Suttafriends.org. Retrieved from: https://suttafriends.org/sutta/thag4-10/

For those who aspire to attain enlightenment, it will be beneficial to practice Dhamma in line with Buddha's original teaching and as a form of training, reflect on non-self-view in daily life and the qualities of Buddha, Dhamma, and noble Sangha to eliminate the first three fetters and to gain the non-self-view. The practice of reflecting non-self-view can be accompanied by reflecting the qualities of Buddha and other practices including loving-kindness meditation and the training rules (or precepts) to suit personal preferences and needs.

CHAPTER TWENTY:
STREAM ENTRY AND BEYOND

Those who attain stream entry will possess perfect confidence in Buddha, Dhamma, and noble Sangha, and noble virtues or morals. Therefore, those who want to attain stream-entry will benefit by developing these four qualities. The four factors of a stream-enterer are illustrated in many Suttas in the Pali Canon. See the following quotation, a passage of the Paṭhamagiñjakāvasathasutta as evidence of this matter:

"And what is that mirror of the teaching?

It's when a noble disciple has experiential confidence in the Buddha ... the teaching ... the Saṅgha ... And they have the ethical conduct loved by the noble ones ... leading to immersion. This is that mirror of the teaching. A noble disciple who has this may declare of themselves: 'I've finished with rebirth in hell, the animal realm, and the ghost realm. I've finished with all places of loss, bad places, the underworld. I am a stream-enterer! I'm not liable to be reborn in the underworld, and am bound for awakening[93]."

- SN 55.8 (Paṭhamagiñjakāvasathasutta)

A passage of the Dīghāvuupāsaka Sutta summarises as:

"In that case, Dīghāvu, grounded on these four factors of stream-entry you should further develop these six things that play a part in realiza-

---

[93] Ref: "Paṭhamagiñjakāvasathasutta: In the Brick Hall (1st)", SN 55.8, (Translated from Pali by Bhikku Sujato), Linked Discourses 55, SuttaCentral.net. Retrieved from: https://suttacentral.net/sn55.8/en/sujato

tion. You should meditate observing the impermanence of all conditions, perceiving suffering in impermanence, perceiving not-self in suffering, perceiving giving up, perceiving fading away, and perceiving cessation. That's how you should train." [94]."

- SN 55.3 (Dīghāvuupāsakasutta)

A passage of the Gihisutta summarises as:

"You should know, Sariputta, that any white-robed house-holder whose actions are restrained by these five training rules and who gains at will, without trouble or difficulty, these four pleasant visible dwellings that pertain to the higher mind, might, if he so wished, declare of himself: I am finished with hell, the animal realm , and the sphere of afflicted spirits; I am finished with the plane of misery, the bad destination, the lower world; I am a stream -enterer, no longer subject to [rebirth in] the lower world, fixed in destiny, heading for enlightenment."[95]

- AN 5.179 (Gihisutta)

Dhammapada Verse 164 and Story record as:

"Once in Savatthi, an elderly woman was looking after a Thera named Kala, like her own son. One day hearing from her neighbours about the virtues of the Buddha, she wished very much to go to the Jetavana monastery and listen to the discourses given by the Buddha. So she told Thera Kala about her wishes; but the thera advised her against it. Three times she spoke to him about her wishes but he always dissuaded her. But one day, in spite of his dissuasion, the lady decided to go. After asking her daughter to look to the needs of Thera Kala she left the house. When Thera Kala came on his usual round of almsfood, he learned that the lady of the house had left for the Jetavana monastery. Then he reflected, "It is quite possible that the lady of this

---

[94] Ref: "Dīghāvuupāsakasutta: With Dīghāvu", Translated by Bhikkhu Sujato, SN 55.3, Linked Discourses 55, SuttaCentral.net. Retrieved from: https://suttacentral.net/sn55.3/en/sujato
[95] Bhikkhu Bodhi (2012), AN 5.179, *A Layman*, p.793.

house is losing her faith in me." So, he made haste and quickly followed her to the monastery. There, he found her listening to the discourse being given by the Buddha. He approached the Buddha respectfully, and said, "Venerable Sir! This woman is very dull; she will not be able to understand the sublime Dhamma; please teach her only about charity (dana) and morality (sila)."

The Buddha knew very well that Thera Kala was talking out of spite and with an ulterior motive. So he said to Thera Kala, 'Bhikkhu! Because you are foolish and because of your wrong view, you scorn my Teaching. You yourself are your own ruin; in fact, you are only trying to destroy yourself.'

Then the Buddha spoke in verse as follows:

Verse 164: The foolish man who, on account of his wrong views, scorns the teaching of homage-worthy Noble Ones (Ariyas) who live according to the Dhamma is like the bamboo which bears fruit for its own destruction.

At the end of the discourse the elderly lady attained Sotapatti Fruition[96]."
- Dhammapada Verse 164

Buddha's teaching is open to people from all backgrounds and it is possible to attain enlightenment with the right Dhamma practice. A passage of the Suddhika Sutta summarises as:

"Regardless of whether one is a royal caste person, or a brahmin high caste person, merchant, worker, an outcast or an untouchable, if he is energetic and dedicated to the Dhamma path, always firm in striving, he will attain the highest happiness, Nibbāna. Know that for a fact, Suddhika[97]."

- SN 7.7 (Suddhika Sutta)

---

[96] Ref: Daw Mya Tin, (1986), The Dhammapada: Verses and Stories.
[97] Ref: "Suddhika Sutta: Suddhika", Brahmaṇa Saṁyutta, Kiribathgoda Ganananda Thero (2017), Suttafriends.org. Retrieved from: https://suttafriends.org/sutta/sn7-7/

As pointed out by Buddha, the purpose of Dhamma practice should be to attain enlightenment. A passage of the Mahāsāropamasutta summarises as:

"So this holy life, bhikkhus, does not have gain, honour, and renown for its benefit, or the attainment of virtue for its benefit, or the attainment of concentration for its benefit, or knowledge and vision for its benefit. But it is this unshakeable deliverance of mind that is the goal of this holy life, its heart-wood, and its end[98]".

-MN 29 (Mahāsāropamasutta)

A passage of the Gārava Sutta summarises as:

"All the Buddhas who lived, will live, and live now, regarded the Dhamma as their teacher, deeply respecting it. This is a natural law for all the Buddhas. Therefore, the person desiring his own good, wishing for great spiritual growth, should deeply respect the Supreme Dhamma, recollecting the Buddha's training[99]."

- SN 6.2 (Gārava Sutta)

---

[98] Ref: "Mahāsāropamasutta: The Greater Discourse on the Simile of the Heartwood", MN 29, translated by Bhikkhu Bodhi, Suttacentral.net, Retrieved from: https://suttacentral.net/mn29/en/bodhi

[99] Ref: "Gārava Sutta: The Discourse on Honoring the Teacher", SN 6.2, Brahma Saṁyutta, Kiribathgoda Ganananda Thero (2017), Suttafriends.org. Retrieved from: https://suttafriends.org/sutta/sn6-2

CHAPTER TWENTY-ONE:
ARAHATHSHIP

Arahathship indicates a purity in one's mind. Purity in mind becomes a possibility for those who have attained enlightenment due to insight knowledge of non-self-view.

The Dhammapada Verse 398 summarises as:

"Him I call a brahmana, who has cut the strap (of ill will), the thong (of craving) and the cord (of wrong views together with latent defilements), who has lifted the bar that fastens the door (of ignorance), and who knows the Truth[100]"*

- Dhammapada Verse 398

A passage of the Bhabba Sutta summarises as:

"Monks, one who hasn't abandoned nine things is incapable of realizing arahantship. Which nine? Passion, aversion, delusion, anger, resentment, arrogance, insolence, envy, & stinginess. One who hasn't abandoned these nine things is incapable of realizing arahantship.

"One who has abandoned nine things is capable of realizing arahantship. Which nine? Passion, aversion, delusion, anger, resentment, arrogance, insolence, envy, & stinginess. One who has abandoned these nine things is capable of realizing arahantship[101]."

- AN 9.62 (Bhabba Sutta)

---

[100] *The word brahmana means Arahanth.
Ref: Daw Mya Tin, (1986), The Dhammapada: Verses and Stories.
[101] Ref: "Bhabba Sutta: Capable", AN 9.62, translated by Ṭhānissaro Bhikkhu, dhammatalks.org. Retrieved from: https://www.dhammatalks.org/suttas/AN/AN9_62.html

A passage of the Vatthasutta summarises as:

"Bhikkhus, suppose a cloth were pure and bright, and a dyer dipped it in some dye or other, whether blue or yellow or red or carmine; it would look well dyed and pure in colour. Why is that? Because of the purity of the cloth. So too, when the mind is undefiled, a happy destination may be expected[102]".

- MN 7 (Vatthasutta)

A passage of the Theragāthā summarises as:

"I understood the suffering of the five aggregates of clinging completely. My craving has been completely rooted out. The Enlightenment Factors have been developed by me. I have attained enlightenment."

"Because I completely understood the suffering of the five aggregates of clinging, craving has been completely rooted out and the Enlightenment Factors have been developed by me. I will attain final extinguishing at passing away without taints[103]".

- The Verses of Arahant Uttara (Thag 2.21)

Initially, it may appear that it's a hard thing to get rid of all nine things to become an Arahanth. If one tries to eradicate above nine things completely (as in AN 9:62) while maintaining the self-view, it becomes a hard thing to do in practice or it becomes impossible. However, if one tries to eliminate these nine things by gaining the non-self-view through insight, it becomes possible to eradicate these nine things (and develop enlightenment factors) to become an Arahanth.

Therefore, one who aspire to achieve enlightenment requires to eliminate self-view first. As a consequence of understanding non-self-

---

[102] Ref: "Vatthasutta: The Simile of the Cloth", MN 7, translated by Bhikkhu Bodhi, Suttacentral.net. Retrieved from: https://suttacentral.net/mn7/en/bodhi
[103] Ref: The Verses of Arahant Uttara, Thag 2.21, Thag 2, Theragāthā, Kiribathgoda Gananananda Thero (2017), Suttafriends.org. Retrieved from: https://suttafriends.org/sutta/thag2-1/

view, the rest nine things will be naturally eradicated in an individual's mind, and the path to enlightenment becomes a comfortable middle way.

Non self-view is gained at the first stage of enlightenment (Sotapanna). Although time may vary between individuals, one who attains the first stage of enlightenment is certain to become an Arahant and to experience the blissful Nibbana within. By following the teachings of Buddha as proclaimed by him, one can realise Arahathship.

CHAPTER TWENTY-TWO:
Further Thoughts

A few key aspects related to attaining enlightenment are discussed in this book and are illustrated in a way that readers can easily comprehend. Below is the summary of these key issues.

First, Dhamma is to be practiced in real life every day. By practicing Dhamma diligently, one can gain success both materialistically and spiritually. By performing wholesome deeds, maintaining virtues and fulfilling responsibilities in life towards others with love and compassion, one can be successful in all areas of life materialistically and also experience inner peace and attain enlightenment.

Second, enlightenment is achieved through four progressive stages (Sotapanna, Sakadagami, Anagami and Arahant). Listening to Dhamma from a person who has attained enlightenment (a noble person) is helpful to developing the right vision. This is because noble people can share their direct experiences. One can attain enlightenment by paying careful attention to Dhamma and practicing in line with Buddha's teaching.

Third, the Buddha's disciples included in the Triple Gem are those individuals who have experienced enlightenment at four stages (in Pali: Sotapanna, Sakadagami, Anagami, and Arahant). This means the four types of noble disciples (or the eight types as individual types including those who are on the path to enlightenment) are the true disciples of Buddha or the Sangha that included in the Triple gem.

Fourth, Buddha has appreciated the wise realization of Dhamma and the inner qualities of a person that makes one a noble character and not the external factors such as robe, dwelling or background. People from any background can attain enlightenment, and Buddha's teaching is open to all irrespective of lay or monastic, young or old, men or women; all can attain enlightenment if they follow Buddha's teaching in the way that he proclaimed. Given that enlightenment is happening at the mental level, the outside appearance or physical location or dwelling and related factors are not contributory factors. Noble Sangha (or Ariyas) comes from any setting.

Fifth, Jhana practiced in line with the precise instructions of the Buddha will lead to enlightenment, because the concentrative state (jhana) should be developed alongside the right view to attain the enlightenment. Right view is gained at the first stage of enlightenment, and three fetters are at once abandoned. Right view is gained by gaining the non-self-view and by removing the doubts about Buddha and his teachings. Thereby not mixing outsiders' teaching into Buddha's teaching along with non-self-view are essential for the attainment of enlightenment.

Sixth, one abandons ten fetters during the process of enlightenment. At the first stage of enlightenment, one abandons the self-view (along with doubts about Buddha, his teachings and his noble disciples). The insight of non-self-view gained at the first stage of enlightenment will naturally drive one toward attaining the Arahathship, subject to a maximum of 7 rebirths at the utmost. Thus, for those who aspire to attain enlightenment, it will be beneficial to put extra effort into attaining the first stage of enlightenment or Sotapanna by practicing Dhamma diligently and in line with Buddha's original teachings.

In terms of training methods, initially, in the path towards the first stage of enlightenment, one must observe the precepts or training rules, because practicing precepts allows one to develop concentration that will lead to the wisdom that requires investigating the teachings of Buddha (or Dhamma). Once one attains the stage of Sotapanna, the importance of precepts diminishes, because one naturally behaves with morals consistent with insight and precepts. Consequently, precepts or training rules are no longer needed, which is particularly applicable for those who have attained the higher stages of enlightenment. Initially, trying to be a good person by fulfilling one's responsibilities toward others will be a helpful factor in attaining the stages of enlightenment. While engaging in and performing wholesome and meritorious activities in daily life, one should engage in further training related to reflecting the qualities of Buddha. One should begin reflecting the qualities of Buddha as a form of meditation to eliminate the first three fetters. Similarly, one can combine the practice of reflecting the qualities of Triple Gem with non-self-view as a form of meditation. To attain the third stage of enlightenment (Anagami), it is beneficial to engage in mindfulness meditation (MN 10) to eliminate the root of sensual desires. The one who attains the first stage of enlightenment is guaranteed to attain the fourth stage eventually and become an Arahant. To conclude, it is possible to attain enlightenment by following Buddha's teachings.

SOURCES

Bhikku Bodhi (2012), The numerical Discourses of the Buddha, A translation of the Anguttara Nikaya, Wisdom Publications, Boston. *(Digital source retrieved from: http://lirs.ru/lib/sutra/The_Numerical_Discourses_of_the_Buddha,Anguttara_Nikaya,Bodhi,2012.pdf) (Last Accessed 31.08.21)*

Bhikkhu Nanamoli and Bhikkhu Bodhi (Translated from the Pali by Bikku Nanamoli and Edited and Revised by Bhikku Bodhi) (1995), A new Translation of the Majjima Nikaya, Buddhist Publication Society, Kandy. *(Digital source retrieved from: http://lirs.ru/lib/sutra/The_Middle_Length_Discourses(Majjhima_Nikaya),Nanamoli,Bodhi,1995.pdf) (Last Accessed 31.08.21)*

Daw Mya Tin, M. A. (1986). The Dhammapada: Verses and Stories, (1986), Edited by Editorial Committee, Burma Tipitaka , Association Rangoon, Burma, (Courtesy of Nibbana.com). *(Digital source retrieved from: https://tienvnguyen.net/images/file/kx6TZFiS0ggQAEMp/dhammapada-versesandstories-a.pdf (Last Accessed 02.09.21)*

Web Sources

Access to Insight (*Contributing Authors include "Amaravati Sangha", 2008)*

https://www.accesstoinsight.org

Dhammatalks.org. *(Suttas from the Pāli Canon translated by Ṭhānissaro Bhikkhu (2017).*

https://www.dhammatalks.org

SuttaCentral.net. *(Suttas from the Pāli Canon translated by Bhikkhu Sujato (2018), primary source was the digital Mahāsaṅgīti edition of the Pali Tipiṭaka).*

https://suttacentral.net

SuttaFriends.org *(Based on the Sinhala translations by Kiribathgoda Gnanananda Thero (2017).*

https://suttafriends.org

May all beings be well and happy.

www.ingramcontent.com/pod-product-compliance
Lightning Source LLC
LaVergne TN
LVHW061344080526
838199LV00094B/7349